Quantity
discount program

The POCKET GUIDE TO FINANCIAL PRODUCTS AND SERVICES is an essential resource for every financial institution employee. Detailing a full range of banking and financial products and services, it places product information, customer profiles and cross-selling checklists at your fingertips. Using THE POCKET GUIDE will help you effectively target new customers and build relationships with established patrons.

A special quantity discount is available when ordering 10 or more copies!

In addition to the discounted price, with an order of 10 or more copies you will receive a complimentary copy of TRAINER'S RESOURCE MANUAL. The manual is an invaluable aid in planning effective in-house training—for either group or individualized sessions—based on THE POCKET GUIDE. With step-by-step descriptions of training sessions, quizzes and exercises, TRAINER'S RESOURCE MANUAL is an excellent reference for every trainer and manager.

For quantity discounts and other information about THE POCKET GUIDE TO FINANCIAL PRODUCTS AND SERVICES (ISBN: 0-7863-1110-X) or the TRAINER'S RESOURCE MANUAL (ISBN: 0-7863-1109-6) call Irwin Professional Publishing, Customer Service at (800) 634-3966 ext. 2460.

THE POCKET GUIDE TO FINANCIAL PRODUCTS AND SERVICES

➤ Product Information

➤ Customer Profiles

➤ Cross-Selling Checklist

Dwight S. Ritter

IRWIN
Professional Publishing®

Chicago • London • Singapore

© Richard D. Irwin, a Times Mirror Higher Education Group, Inc. company, 1997

All rights reserved. No part of this publication may be reproduced, stored in a retrieval system, or transmitted, in any form or by any means, electronic, mechanical, photocopying, recording, or otherwise, without the prior written permission of the publisher and the authors.

This publication is designed to provide accurate and authoritative information in regard to the subject matter covered. It is sold with the understanding that the author and the publisher are not engaged in rendering legal, accounting, or other professional service. If legal advice or other expert assistance is required, the services of a competent professional person should be sought.

From a Declaration of Principles jointly adopted by a Committee of the American Bar Association and a Committee of Publishers.

Times Mirror
Higher Education Group

Printed in the United States of America
1 2 3 4 5 6 7 8 9 0 DO 3 2 1 0 9 8 7 6

About the Author

Dwight S. Ritter is the founder and Chief Executive Officer of The Ritter Company, a management and marketing consulting company specializing in the financial and fiduciary services industry worldwide. His client list encompasses more than 1,000 banks, mutual funds, trust companies, law firms, and accounting firms in the United States and many of the major banks, private bankers, and trust companies of Europe, the Caribbean, and Latin America. With a diverse client list which includes such institutions as Bank of Boston, Wells Fargo, National Commerce Bank Services, Fidelity Investments, Bank of Ireland, Citco Bank (Amsterdam), First National Bank of Aruba, Curacao International Trust Company, Poncebank, and others, Mr. Ritter's breadth of knowledge within the financial and fiduciary services industry spans everything from supermarket banking to foreign sales corporations, commercial lending, and international trust agreements.

About *The Pocket Guide to Financial Products and Services*

This pocket guide has been designed for the financial and fiduciary services sales professional. Its objectives are:

- → To provide a thorough definition of many financial and fiduciary services.

- → To define the user of these services.

- → To provide a ranked listing of related services that present an opportunity for cross-selling.

How to Use This Pocket Guide

This pocket guide is based on the concept of "lead product selling," a business practice fast gaining acceptance in today's financial and fiduciary services industry. This concept actually began in small savings banks, where bankers, under pressure to compete with the growing financial services industry, realized two sure-fire ways to attract, keep, and increase customers. First, bankers noticed that the more products they could place with a customer, the lower was the probability that the customer would leave the bank. Second, bankers observed that the more products they placed with a customer, the more profitable that total banking relationship would be. Thus, the practice of lead product selling, which refers to the first product a customer asks for, created an opportunity for bankers to sell many ancillary, fee-based products that would have been very difficult to sell on their own (as a lead product).

There are numerous examples of how to implement the practice of lead product selling, or cross-selling, in a variety of financial and fiduciary services:

- When a banker working in retail banking, at the branch level, meets with a customer who asks about a checking (or current) account, the banker should sell **off of** that checking account.

- When a commercial lender meets with a large business to discuss a revolving line of credit, that commercial officer should know that he or she can **cross sell** commercial loans, employee direct deposits, or a variety of cash management services **off of** that revolving line of credit.

- The trust officer in the Caribbean who is working with a client interested in opening an International Business Corporation (IBC) knows that there might be an opportunity to **cross sell** ship registration and a variety of depository services.

- Even the stockbroker must realize, in the beginning, that selling money market accounts, cash reserves, credit cards, and estate and trust work is part of his or her job. If a customer wants to open a money market account, then it is incumbent upon the stockbroker to suggest, for example, other kinds of investments or investment services.

In several meetings with the editorial committee formed to oversee this guide, we defined two to three times the number of products and services we finally settled on. Also, we argued at great length about which products and services were related to the lead product, as well as the sequence of those products and services. We welcome comments from practitioners using this guide and input to improve the contents.

All astute marketing/sales professionals should carry this guide with them. When discussing a specific service with a client, it would be quite appropriate to look up that service in this guide and to take note of any related services that would provide your client with supportive opportunities.

At the end of this guide are several helpful sales aids which allow you to assist your customers in a knowledgeable and professional way. The *1996-1997 Global Economic Outlook* chart is a monthly chart that you must keep up to date; especially if you deal with customers who conduct business in more than one country. The *Global Economic Outlook* will illustrate trends in five (5) distinct categories, measuring a country's economic ups and downs. Finding the numbers to put in the monthly boxes is easy. GNP, unemployment, etc., are all listed in most of the international newspapers. *The Wall Street Journal* posts each indicator in the U.S. on a published list.

Finally, in the back of this guide, you will find an interesting essay on the issue of confidentiality in banking.

Table of Contents

About the Author v

About *The Pocket Guide to
Financial Products & Services* vii

How to Use This Pocket Guide ix

Cross-Selling Tools 1

Appendix 211

    Confidentiality 212

    1996–1997 Global Economic Outlook 214

    Market Trends:
    Illustrative Annual Rates of Return 218

Index 221

Other Business-Related
Books by Dwight S. Ritter 242

Cross-Selling Tools

Account Analysis

A way to maximize earnings allowance credits by combining balances in multiple business accounts, This procedure usually results in an offset to high service charges in the accounts.

Banks typically generate analysis statements that summarize a customer's account activity and use of miscellaneous services. These analyses can be issued monthly, quarterly, semi-annually, or annually.

The bank can either assess the account for service charges in excess of earnings credit or directly bill customers for the analysis.

The Customer

Financial officers, bookkeepers for companies.

Cross Sell:
Account Analysis

➤ Money Market Deposit Account
To enable a business to earn interest on excess funds

➤ Sweep Investment Account
To sweep excess funds to a higher-earning investment account

➤ Business Credit Line
As a quick way to borrow funds

➤ Credit Card
To control travel and entertainment expense

➤ Notes

Contacts	Department	Telephone

Pricing/Fees _____

_____

_____

Miscellaneous _____

_____

_____

Account Reconciliation

A commercial banking service for reconciling statements and checks, enabling customers who handle large numbers of checks to control items paid and items outstanding.

This service is typically offered with two options:

Full Account Reconciliation: With this option, a customer submits a record of each outstanding item issued, furnishing either a magnetic tape or a copy of all MICR-encoded items for capture. A matching report compares serially sorted checks/items paid against outstanding items captured; all remaining, uncleared items are printed out separately. Cut-offs for settlement can be weekly, bimonthly, or monthly.

Partial Account Reconciliation: Only cleared checks are serially sorted for the matching report. Outstanding items are not included in the matching report.

In addition to a monthly fee, payment for this service includes fees for check sorting, tape input, and MICR input.

The Customer

Financial officers, bookkeepers for companies.

Cross Sell:
Account Reconciliation

➛ Money Market or Checking (Current) Account
As a convenient way to keep an accurate record of cash flow

➛ Sweep Investment Account
To sweep excess funds to a higher-earning investment account

➛ Business Credit Line
As a quick way to borrow funds

➛ Payroll Direct Deposit
As an easy, hassle-free way to deposit employees' paychecks

➛ Credit Card
To control travel and entertainment expense

→ Notes

Contacts	Department	Telephone

Pricing/Fees _____

_____

_____

Miscellaneous_____

_____

_____

Acting as Trustee

The legal function of performing specified fiduciary tasks in connection with assisting and/or managing the activities of a trust. Acting as Trustee can be performed by anyone so authorized; most often, though, this service is provided by an attorney or a trust officer.

The Customer

Individuals needing trust services, corporate officers managing corporate trusts, attorneys.

Cross Sell:
Acting as Trustee

➤ Trust Services
For access to a wide range of advice and counsel on financial and fiduciary matters

➤ Estate Planning
To assist in overall family financial planning

➤ Portfolio Management
To assist in investment strategies and execution

➤ Checking (Current) Account
To provide depository for short-term funds

➤ Brokerage Services
For trading in the securities market

➤ Margin Account
To maximize use of equity buying

➤ Mutual Funds
To offer a variety of risk levels and returns for the hands-on investor

➤ Legal Services
To assist with trusts, wills, and certain tax matters

➤ Foreign Sales Corporation (FSC) or International Business Corporation (IBC)
For the administration and management of tax-protected holdings

---

➤ Notes

Contacts	Department	Telephone

Pricing/Fees _____

Miscellaneous _____

Adjustable Rate Mortgages (ARMs)

A mortgage on which the rate is adjusted periodically over the life of the loan. Rate and monthly payments will vary depending on what happens to interest rates in general.

ARMs are available in the following forms:

- One-Year ARM—rate changes every year.
- Three-Year ARM—rate changes once every three years.
- Five/One ARM—rate fixed for first five years, then adjusts annually thereafter.

This type of mortgage features a rate cap that limits the maximum amount the mortgage rate can change during each adjustment period, as well as over the life of the loan. The rate on an ARM is tied to an established index and a margin that is constant.

ARMs are popular with certain types of customers because they have lower initial rates and monthly payments than do fixed-rate mortgages. In addition, lower payments allow borrowers to qualify for larger loans. Offsetting the advantage of lower rates, however, is the risk of the rate going up, prompting monthly payments to increase.

The Customer

Usually more transient customers than those seeking a fixed-rate mortgage: younger, working for a large company, frequent mover. Older customers are usually purchasing for a short term until retirement.

Cross Sell:
Adjustable Rate Mortgages (ARMs)

⇾ Insurance
To pay off the mortgage in the event of the mortgagee's death

⇾ Equity Line of Credit
As a convenient, tax-advantaged way to make significant purchases

⇾ Checking (Current) Account
As a convenient way to make mortgage payments

⇾ Automatic Payment
As a more convenient way than checking for making mortgage payments

---

➤ Notes

Contacts	Department	Telephone

Pricing/Fees _____

_____

_____

Miscellaneous _____

_____

_____

Aggressive Growth Fund

A high-risk mutual fund that invests in the common stock of young or start-up companies and industries, or in "out-of-favor" companies or industries. The objective of this type of mutual fund is to achieve the maximum increase in total return.

The Customer

Investors who don't want to spend the time (or take the chance) buying and selling stocks, bonds, Certificates of Deposit (CDs), or Treasury Bills, but who nevertheless are still willing to pursue high-risk investments.

Cross Sell:
Aggressive Growth Fund

➤ Deposit Account
(Checking, Money Market, or fund with checkbook)
To accept dividends or income and to buy other investments

➤ Margin Account
To buy when the research is convincing, regardless of the deposit account balance

➤ Credit Card
For travel, entertainment, and special purchases

➤ Retirement Account
To accept maximum contributions as defined by law

➤ Trust Services
For expertise in estate planning and investments

➤ Notes

Contacts	Department	Telephone

Pricing/Fees _____

_____

_____

Miscellaneous _____

_____

_____

Annuities

A savings/retirement product offered through insurance companies. This product allows a scheduled withdrawal of principal and interest, based on life expectancy tables or on tax-deferred buildup.

Annuities are purchased by individuals focusing on long-range planning of their retirement proceeds. The interest from annuities is tax-deferred and the payout is fixed, regardless of future interest rates.

Although most insurance companies offer a variety of annuities, these products generally come in two forms:

- A Tax-Deferred Annuity requires a minimum investment. Interest on the principal is tax-deferred and can be annuitized. There is a penalty for early withdrawal.

- An Immediate Annuity requires a larger minimum investment than a standard, tax-deferred annuity. Here, the annuitant immediately begins receiving scheduled payments as "tax-advantaged" payouts, versus those of other traditional retirement products. Individual Retirement Account (IRA) funds can be used for immediate annuities.

The Customer

Most often individuals close to retirement age who have not put aside quite enough retirement money and therefore need to annuitize their holdings.

Cross Sell: Annuities

→ Certificates of Deposit (CDs) or Time Deposits
A low-risk place for invested funds

→ Individual Retirement Account (IRA)
As a tax-deferred shelter for the customer who hasn't put aside enough retirement money

→ Life Insurance
For providing cash value or an annuitized source of retirement income

---

→ Notes

Contacts	Department	Telephone

Pricing/Fees _____

_____

_____

Miscellaneous_____

_____

_____

Asset Allocation Fund

A mutual fund that invests in a mixture of bonds, preferred and common stocks, and short-term debt securities. (See Balanced Fund)

This is a low-risk investment seeking current income, long-term growth, and safety. In some cases this type of fund offers a checkbook and is the recipient of dividend payments and sales of stocks or of other mutual funds.

The Customer

The investment-conscious who don't want to spend the time (or take the chance) buying and selling stocks, bonds, etc.

Cross Sell:
Asset Allocation Fund

↠ Deposit Account
(Checking, Money Market, or fund with checkbook)
To accept dividends or income and to buy other investments

↠ Growth and/or Income Mutual Funds
To receive the investment money from the depository

↠ Brokerage Services
(or Discount Brokerage)
For investment in researched equities

↠ Margin Account
To buy when the research is convincing, regardless of the deposit account balance

↠ Credit Card
For travel, entertainment, and special purchases

↠ Retirement Account
To accept maximum contributions as defined by law

↠ Trust Services
For expertise in estate planning and investments

→ Notes

Contacts	Department	Telephone

Pricing/Fees _____

_____

_____

Miscellaneous_____

_____

Asset-Based Lending

A specialized line of credit on which the bank advances funds to a company, usually against a predetermined percentage of its accounts receivable or inventory. In general, loans against inventory are significantly less than the value of the finished products.

Asset-based lines of credit are subject to the same analysis and approval guidelines as other commercial loans. The borrower gives the bank periodic information for the purpose of monitoring the loan, including documentation on the aging of accounts (both receivable and payable), inventory reports, and financial statements.

Before granting this kind of credit line against accounts receivable, the bank closely investigates the company's financial condition and the industry in which it operates. Once the bank advances funds, it periodically audits the company's books and inventory.

The Customer

Most medium-to-large businesses that maintain an inventory. The bank usually works with a company representative who can speak knowledgeably about its financial condition.

Cross Sell:
Asset-Based Lending

➤ Business Checking Account
As a customary prerequisite for a business loan

➤ Line of Credit
To save borrowing time and ensure the availability of funds

➤ Online Balance Reporting
To improve funds management by the monitoring of account balances

➤ Account Analysis
As an easy way to consolidate activity and to improve control with multiple accounts

➤ Direct Deposit
For automatic deposit of employees' paychecks into their accounts

➤ Employee Checking Account
As a convenient way to provide banking services to a company's employees

---

➤ Notes

Contacts	Department	Telephone

Pricing/Fees _____

_____

_____

Miscellaneous _____

_____

_____

Automobile Loans

A standard, fixed-rate, secured loan for an automobile (both new and used models). In the United States, these loans require a 20 percent down payment for cars three to five years old and 10 percent on current models.

These loans are available through both automobile dealers and a range of financial institutions. With the advent of leasing, the demand for traditional, secured automobile loans has been reduced. From a bank's point of view, the secured automobile loan can be a profitable product, but more important, it serves as an opportunity for multiple cross sales.

The Customer

Most persons purchasing a new or used automobile.

Cross Sell:
Automobile Loans

➤ Checking (Current) Account
As a convenient way to keep an accurate record of cash flow

➤ Automatic Teller Machine (ATM)
To access funds at any hour, on any day, at locations worldwide

➤ Automatic Payment
As a more reliable way than checking to pay bills and to ensure a good credit history

➤ Home Equity Line of Credit
To have tax-advantaged funds available for a variety of purposes

---

➤ Notes

Contacts	Department	Telephone

Pricing/Fees _____

_____

_____

Miscellaneous _____

_____

_____

Automatic Teller Machine (ATM) Card

Issued to banking customers who wish to use ATMs for withdrawing cash, for making loan payments, and for depositing checks or cash. Since 1980 these machines have become increasingly standardized, allowing one card to be used in ATMs around the world.

Cirrus, NYCE, Express 24, and a host of other financial networks have made ATMs very convenient and safe to use in thousands of locations throughout the world.

The Customer

Almost anyone who qualifies for a checking account.

Cross Sell:
Automatic Teller Machine (ATM) Card

➤ Checking (Current) Account
As a prerequisite for the ATM card

➤ Overdraft Protection
To prevent an accidental overdraft

➤ Direct Deposit
As an automatic function for the deposit of paychecks or government checks

➤ Savings Account
To link with the checking account via the ATM card

Notes

Contacts	Department	Telephone

Pricing/Fees _____

Miscellaneous _____

Balanced Fund

A mutual fund that invests in a mixture of bonds, preferred stock and common stocks, as well as short-term debt securities. Sometimes referred to as an asset allocation fund, this is a low-risk investment seeking current income, long-term growth, and safety.

In some cases this type of fund offers a checkbook and is the recipient of dividend payments and sales of stocks or other mutual funds.

The Customer

The investment-conscious who don't want to spend the time (or take the chance) buying and selling stocks, bonds, etc.

Cross Sell:
Balanced Fund

➤ Deposit Account
(Checking, Money Market or fund with checkbook)
To accept dividends and income and to buy other investments

➤ Growth and/or Income Mutual Funds
To receive the investment money from the depository

➤ Brokerage Services
(or Discount Brokerage)
For investment in researched equities

➤ Margin Account
To buy when the research is convincing, regardless of the deposit account balance

➤ Credit Card
For travel, entertainment, and special purchases

➤ Retirement Account
To accept maximum contributions as defined by law

➤ Trust Services
For expertise in estate planning and investments

➤ Notes

Contacts	Department	Telephone

Pricing/Fees _____

_____

_____

Miscellaneous _____

_____

Bank-by-Mail

A service offered by most financial institutions, enabling customers to execute their transactions totally by mail.

The Customer

Someone who is very busy and time-conscious. This service also appeals to the ill, disabled, and invalid.

Cross Sell:
Bank-by-Mail

→ Automatic Teller Machine (ATM)
To access funds at any hour, on any day, at locations worldwide

→ Automatic Payment
To make loan payments without writing checks, thereby saving time

→ Direct Deposit
As a safe, quick way to have paychecks deposited

→ Overdraft Protection
To spare customers the embarrassment of accidental overdraft

→ Equity Credit Line
As a quick, tax-advantaged method of obtaining extra money for significant purchases

---

→ Notes

Contacts	Department	Telephone

Pricing/Fees _____

_____

_____

Miscellaneous _____

_____

_____

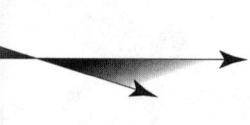

Bonds (Corporate and Municipal)

A loan to a government or corporation for repayment on a specified date. Government bonds are used to build or rebuild the domestic infrastructure and therefore cannot offer equity. Corporate bonds are one of various ways that corporations raise money for specific reasons.

All bonds are similar in three respects: they are repaid at a specified interest rate, at a specified date, and for a specified amount.

Bond values are mainly measured by a yield, which is the interest rate the bond pays as earnings. The yield is determined by a simple calculation—dividing the amount of money a bond will pay in interest by the price of the bond.

The yield on bonds has historically been very predictable (since it is, after all, a loan), and many retirees have opted for this predictability. In addition, bonds have been considered a more conservative investment than the unpredictable equities.

The Customer

Any investor can be a bond customer, particularly those who want safe investments.

Cross Sell:
Bonds (Corporate and Municipal)

➔ Stocks
(Equities)
To diversify one's investments

➔ Bond Mutual Funds
As a less risky approach than investing in bonds individually

➔ Stock Mutual Funds
To add diversity to one's portfolio

➔ Money Market Account
A depository for cash from investments

➔ Credit Card
To document travel and entertainment expenses

➤ Notes

Contacts	Department	Telephone

Pricing/Fees _____

_____

_____

Miscellaneous_____

_____

_____

Bond Mutual Funds

A mutual fund that invests in a broad range of bonds, from corporate to government. These funds increase and decrease in their net asset value in direct disproportion to the interest rates. Their fluctuations, however, are not as extreme (as a general rule) as the fluctuations in growth or growth-and-income equity funds.

In some cases this type of fund offers a checkbook and is the recipient of dividend payments and sales of stocks or other mutual funds.

The Customer

The investment-conscious who are interested in creating a diverse portfolio.

Cross Sell:
Bond Mutual Funds

→ **Deposit Account**
(Checking, Money Market or fund with checkbook)
To accept dividends and income and to buy other investments

→ **Growth and/or Income Mutual Funds**
To diversify the customer's holdings

→ **Brokerage Services**
(or Discount Brokerage)
for investment in researched equities

→ **Margin Account**
To buy when the research is convincing, regardless of the deposit account balance

→ **Credit Card**
For travel, entertainment, and special purchases

→ **Retirement Account**
To accept maximum contributions as defined by law

→ **Trust Services**
For expertise in estate planning and investments

➤ Notes

Contacts	Department	Telephone

Pricing/Fees _____

_____

_____

Miscellaneous _____

_____

Brokerage Services

This includes a wide range of investment services available through a number of distribution outlets, for example:

- Stockbrokers buy and sell equities and bonds through their trading institutions. They charge commissions on the buying and selling of these investments (somewhere around 3 percent to buy and 3 percent to sell, depending on the size of the transaction) and offer advice and recommendations on trades.

- Discount brokers also buy and sell equities and bonds through their trading institutions; however, they do not offer advice or make recommendations on trades. Many discount brokers provide touch-tone telephone trading service, which allows the customer to buy and sell without ever speaking to a human! The range of commissions for discount brokers varies tremendously, depending on the amount of the transaction.

- Trust companies, private banks, and some niche players in the financial and fiduciary services business also provide brokerage services. Most of these institutions either buy through a wholesale service similar to a discount broker or have one or more licensed brokers on staff who can make the trades.

The Customer

Investment-oriented and/or high-net-worth individuals, companies, trusts, etc.

Cross Sell: Brokerage Services

➤ Estate Planning
To assist in overall family financial planning

➤ Trust Services
For expertise in the area of investments and planning

➤ Portfolio Management
To assist in investment strategies and execution

➤ Mutual Funds
To offer a variety of risk levels and returns for the hands-on investor

➤ Legal Services
To assist with trusts, wills, and certain tax matters

➤ Checking (Current) Account
As a convenient way to keep an accurate record of cash flow

➤ Automatic Teller Machine (ATM)
To access funds at any hour, on any day, at locations worldwide

---

➤ Notes

Contacts	Department	Telephone

Pricing/Fees _____

_____

_____

Miscellaneous_____

_____

Business Checking Account

A deposit account for businesses that provides check writing and monthly statements that list all activity—deposits, withdrawals, checks, and fees—in the account. Depending on the average daily balance held in these accounts, many of the fees can be waived.

These accounts are also supplied with checks conducive to standard business practices. The checks are furnished to the customer as one-write systems or in computer-generated formats.

A business checking (current) account is a convenient, low-cost account for processing deposits and checks. It is designed for easy account reconciliation.

The Customer

All business owners or financial officers.

Cross Sell:
Business Checking Account

➤ Automatic Teller Machine (ATM)
To access funds and deposits any hour, any day

➤ Commercial Loan
To improve growth through carefully advised lending

➤ Line of Credit
To save borrowing time and improve accounts payable

➤ Business Money Market Account
To function as a Sweep Account for business checking, for the purpose of earning higher interest

➤ Credit Card
For travel and related expenses

➤ Notes

Contacts	Department	Telephone

Pricing/Fees _____

Miscellaneous _____

Business Money Market Account

A business checking account that offers money market rates on the unused balance if the balance exceeds the bank's limit. Balances below the bank's limit generally receive only the NOW rate. Limited check writing is another feature of this account, as are limited telephone transfers.

With most business money market accounts, a maintenance fee is charged and all balances earn interest. This allows businesses to earn interest on excess, unused funds.

The Customer

A business owner or financial officer who is very concerned about maximizing income from all sources.

Cross Sell:
Business Money Market Account

↠ Automatic Teller Machine (ATM)
To access funds and deposits at any hour, on any day

↠ Commercial Loan
To improve growth through carefully advised lending

↠ Line of Credit
To save borrowing time and improve accounts payable

↠ Credit Card
For travel and related expenses

➤ Notes

Contacts	Department	Telephone

Pricing/Fees _____

_____

_____

Miscellaneous _____

_____

_____

Certificates of Deposit (CDs)

An FDIC-insured, time deposit investment that protects principal and provides a guaranteed return. A CD is closely tied to United States interest rates and therefore has a low return when inflation is low but a high return when inflation is high. In the early '80s, interest on CDs was as high as 18 percent!

Many financial institutions offer variations on this product. The most common is a regular CD that comes with a one-time option to "bump-up" to a higher current rate of interest. When interest rates are very low and expected to rise, this can be an attractive option—hedging for the future.

The Customer

Individuals who are concerned about the safety of their investment—in other words, no-risk investors.

Cross Sell:
Certificates of Deposit (CDs)

⇢ Checking (Current) Account
To have an account into which customers can deposit the monthly interest from the CD

⇢ Savings Account
As an alternative to checking

⇢ Automatic Teller Machine (ATM)
To access funds at any hour, on any day, at locations worldwide

⇢ Overdraft Protection
To prevent the expense of an accidental overdraft

⇢ Mutual Funds
For investing a portion of savings at a slightly higher level of risk

---

➤ Notes

Contacts	Department	Telephone

Pricing/Fees _____

_____

_____

Miscellaneous _____

_____

_____

Checking (Current) Account

This is the primary deposit account. Outside the United States, it is referred to as a Current Account. It is a basic, non-interest-bearing account into which one deposits monies for the purpose of writing checks. On a monthly basis the financial institution into which the monies are deposited provides customers with a statement that lists their account activity—deposits, checks written, and service charges. Additionally, checking (current) accounts accept direct deposits and automatic withdrawals, such as insurance premium payments, car and mortgage payments, etc.

Over the years this account has taken on many forms, offering such attractive features as varying the minimum balances required, varying the maintenance and check writing fees, and varying the deposit charges.

The monthly statement provides record-keeping data for tax purposes, as well as routine maintenance of household expenses.

The Customer

Any employed individual who needs some financial management in his or her life.

Cross Sell:
Checking (Current) Account

→ Automatic Teller Machine (ATM)
To access deposited funds at any hour, on any day, at locations worldwide

→ Direct Deposit
As a safe, quick way to have paychecks deposited into a checking account

→ Overdraft Protection
To save customers the embarrassment and expense of accidental overdraft

→ Statement Savings
To link checking to savings via the ATM card

➤ Notes

Contacts	Department	Telephone

Pricing/Fees _____

Miscellaneous _____

Christmas Club

A statement or passbook savings account set up to accept scheduled deposits that will be withdrawn prior to the holiday season. These accounts are traditionally regarded as a disciplined way to set aside cash for holiday shopping.

The Customer

Older people, who long ago got into the habit of using these clubs to help them save for the holidays. Conscientious blue-collar workers who prefer to use cash rather than credit for gift buying.

Cross Sell:
Christmas Club

→ Checking (Current) Account
As a convenient way to keep an accurate record of cash flow

→ Automatic Teller Machine (ATM)
To access funds at any hour, on any day, at locations worldwide

→ Direct Deposit
As a safe, reliable way to have paychecks deposited without standing in line

→ Automatic Transfer of Funds
As an easy, reliable way of building a holiday fund

➤ Notes

Contacts	Department	Telephone

Pricing/Fees _____

_____

_____

Miscellaneous _____

_____

_____

Commercial Loan

A loan with a maturity of one year or more, for which principal and interest is paid back in regular installments. The typical length of this loan is up to five years, and it is used for equipment purchases, vehicle purchases, refinancing of existing corporate debt, consolidation of various loans, and purchase of fixed assets other than real estate.

Before granting a commercial loan, the bank first must understand the purpose, plan, and sources of loan repayment (at least two sources), adequacy of the collateral, and managerial capability and creditworthiness of the borrower. All loans generally require the personal guarantee of the principal(s) of the borrowing company. During the life of the loan, financial statements of the company and of those personally guaranteeing the loan must be submitted to the bank on at least an annual basis.

The Customer

This loan spans the full spectrum of businesses—large and small. Expect to work with company representatives who can speak knowledgeably about the financial condition of their business.

Cross Sell: Commercial Loan

➜ Business Checking Account
As a typical prerequisite for a commercial loan

➜ Line of Credit
To save borrowing time and ensure the availability of funds

➜ Direct Deposit
To simplify payroll operations with electronic deposit of employees' checks

➜ Employee Checking Account
A convenient, easy way to provide banking services to a company's employees

---

➤ Notes

Contacts	Department	Telephone

Pricing/Fees _____

_____

_____

Miscellaneous _____

_____

_____

Commercial Mortgage

A commercial loan used to finance commercial real estate. Terms for this type of loan generally run for three to five years, feature an amortization schedule of up to twenty years, and are renewable subject to a new review process.

These loans may be secured by such income-producing properties as commercial office buildings, industrial buildings, or residential apartment buildings; moreover, properties may be owned for the borrower's business use or for investment purposes. Most commercial mortgage loans are subject to independent appraisals and environmental site assessment.

Proposals for these loans must be examined with particular attention to the cash flow of the project and/or of the business, and to the character and financial strength of the borrower.

The Customer

A developer or builder: knowledgeable, aggressive, and a risk-taker.

Cross Sell:
Commercial Mortgage

⇢ Business Checking
A convenient way to keep an accurate record of the company's cash flow

⇢ Line of Credit
To save borrowing time and ensure the availability of funds

⇢ Direct Deposit
To have employees' paychecks automatically deposited into their accounts.

⇢ Employee Checking
A convenient way to offer banking services to employees

➤ Notes

Contacts	Department	Telephone

Pricing/Fees _____

_____

_____

Miscellaneous_____

_____

_____

Construction Loan

An interim loan designed for individuals who need to finance the construction of a new primary residence or of a second home.

These loans are typically short-term—six months to one year, long enough to cover the construction of a new home. After closing on a construction loan, the bank sets up an account for advancing funds to cover the costs of each phase of construction that the contractor completes. An inspector from the bank must confirm satisfactory completion of the work before the funds are advanced.

The borrower pays interest only on the funds that have been disbursed during the construction period. After all the funds have been released, the borrower pays interest on the entire amount of the loan.

Before issuing a construction loan, banks require varying types of documentation: building permits, housebuilding plans and specifications, contracts with licensed builders, and checking or savings account statements.

The total amount of a construction loan cannot exceed 80 percent of the lower of appraised value or acquisition cost of the land and of the completed structure, unless mortgage insurance can be obtained.

The Customer

A homebuilder or an individual functioning as the general contractor for a home or building.

Cross Sell:
Construction Loan

→ Checking (Current) Account
To pay the materials and labor costs of the project—usually a prerequisite to the loan

→ Mortgage
As the end result of the construction loan

→ Automatic Payment
As a more convenient way than checking for making loan payments

→ Automatic Teller Machine (ATM)
To use at any hour, on any day, at locations worldwide

➤ Notes

Contacts	Department	Telephone

Pricing/Fees _____

Miscellaneous _____

Custodial Accounts

The safekeeping of an individual's securities, such as stocks and bonds, by a bank's personal trust department or by a trust company. Custodial accounts allow customers to retain full ownership and control of their investments.

The services offered in this type of an account include (but are not restricted to) the following:

- The purchase or sale of securities.
- The collection of dividends and interest on securities.
- Accurate maintenance of records of all income received and all securities transactions.

The Customer

The investment-conscious individual who relies on advice.

Cross Sell:
Custodial Accounts

→ Brokerage Services
For trading in the securities chosen

→ Checking (Current) Account
To provide depository for short-term funds

→ Margin Account
To maximize equity buying

→ Estate Planning
To assist in overall family financial planning

→ Portfolio Management
To assist in investment strategies and execution

→ Mutual Funds
To offer a variety of risk levels and returns for the hands-on investor

→ Legal Services
To assist with trusts, wills, and certain tax matters

→ Notes

Contacts	Department	Telephone

Pricing/Fees _____

_____

_____

Miscellaneous_____

_____

_____

Direct Deposit

A banking service that will automatically, and in many cases instantly, deposit money into a deposit account.

United States government social security checks can be deposited instantly through Electronic Funds Transfer (EFT), as can many paychecks of a corporation to its employees.

In addition, direct deposit can be done manually by a bank—for instance, when a bank deposits, on behalf of an employee, a paycheck it has received by mail from the employer. Even though this service is not as instantaneous as EFT, it is very convenient, as it allows employees to have their checks deposited without the bother of going to a bank.

The Customer

Employees of companies, as well as senior citizens, who want to avoid standing in lines to deposit their checks.

Cross Sell:
Direct Deposit

⇾ Checking (Current) Account
As a prerequisite for direct deposit

⇾ Automatic Teller Machine (ATM)
To further simplify the banking process by making deposited funds available at any hour, on any day, at locations worldwide

⇾ Overdraft Protection
To prevent an accidental overdraft

⇾ Savings Account
To link to the checking account via the ATM card

➤ Notes

Contacts	Department	Telephone

Pricing/Fees _____

_____

_____

Miscellaneous _____

_____

_____

Electronic Banking Interface

An easy-to-use software program that lets companies pay, collect, or transfer funds electronically from their own personal computers.

There are several such software programs whose funds-transfer capabilities include:

- Cash Concentration for transferring funds from accounts at different banks into a central account at one bank.

- Direct Payments that allow companies direct, electronic access to their customers' accounts for the purpose of paying bills, dues, or premiums.

- Automated Invoice Payments to pay, electronically, such regular bills as utilities or vendor invoices.

- Direct Deposit to simplify payroll operations by means of electronic deposit of payroll checks.

Transmission and receipt of funds are Automated Clearing House (ACH) transactions that are originated on a company's personal computer, then transmitted to the bank's computer for routing through ACH networks. These programs also include detailed instructions and prompts to guide the user, as well as online balance reporting for analysis of account balances and activity.

The Customer

Financial officer or bookkeeper with knowledge of computers.

Cross Sell:
Electronic Banking Interface

➻ Online Balance Reporting
To improve funds management through the monitoring of account balances and transaction history

➻ Business Checking
As a convenient way to keep an accurate record of cash flow

➻ Account Analysis
To consolidate activity from multiple accounts for better control

➻ Business Credit Line
To borrow quickly and easily on an as-needed basis

➤ Notes

Contacts	Department	Telephone

Pricing/Fees _____

_____

_____

Miscellaneous_____

_____

_____

Electronic Depository Transfer

The bank can originate Automated Clearing House (ACH) transactions for customers who need to consolidate funds, pay bills electronically, or transfer funds frequently from one bank to the other.

This service is ideal for commercial loan customers who need to deposit funds at their bank in order to meet compensating balance requirements on a loan.

This service is paid for through a monthly fee.

The Customer

A financially sensitive business owner or a financial officer.

Cross Sell:
Electronic Depository Transfer

➤ Online Balance Reporting
To improve funds management by the monitoring of account balances

➤ Business Checking
As a convenient way to keep an accurate record of cash flow

➤ Account Analysis
As an easy way to consolidate activity from multiple accounts for better control

➤ Business Credit Line
(or Revolving Line of Credit)
For borrowing funds on an as-needed basis

➤ Notes

Contacts	Department	Telephone

Pricing/Fees _____

_____

_____

Miscellaneous_____

_____

_____

Employee Benefits Services

A vast array of services designed to meet the investment and administrative needs of companies offering retirement plans to their employees.

There are a variety of plans that have been qualified by the government and are available for implementation:

- Profit Sharing Plan
- Money Purchase Pension Plan
- Defined Benefit Plan
- 401(k) Salary Deferral
- Target Benefit Plan

In providing this service, the bank ensures that the company's legal requirements are met with the necessary documents, administrative support, tax filing, and legal information. A bank's knowledgeable staff, with expertise in employee benefits, compliance, investments, and taxation, helps companies select the plan that best fits their needs. The bank's investment management services can assume management of the contributions made into the plan; trustee services can assume responsibility for the accounting and reporting of all plan transactions, securities settlement, and benefit payments. Custodial services safeguard all assets held in a plan, deposit all contributions, collect and process income generated by the plan's assets, and buy or sell securities. All of these services can be utilized at the direction of the company or as part of an overall plan administration offered by a bank or trust company's employee benefits department.

The Customer

Most medium-to-large businesses. The customer is always a company representative familiar with the company's financial condition and sensitive to retirement and pension issues.

Cross Sell:
Employee Benefits Services

⇾ Business Checking Account
A prerequisite for any cash management or credit relationship

⇾ Line of Credit
To save borrowing time and ensure the availability of funds

⇾ Online Balance Reporting
To improve funds management by monitoring account balances

⇾ Account Analysis
As an easy way to consolidate activity from multiple accounts for better control

⇾ Direct Deposit
To have the paychecks of company employees automatically deposited into their accounts

⇾ Employee Checking Account
As a convenient, easy way to provide banking services to a company's employees

---

➤ Notes

Contacts	Department	Telephone

Pricing/Fees _____

_____

_____

Miscellaneous _____

_____

_____

Estate Settlement Services

A bank can serve in various capacities to assist customers in the settlement of estates.

- As Executor, the bank can supervise the settlement of an individual's estate according to his or her will. The bank can probate the will; collect, inventory, and protect assets; provide asset management during the period of estate administration; file necessary tax returns and pay taxes; and distribute assets according to directions in the will.

- If designated as co-Executor, the bank serves with a family member or a friend to provide the services mentioned above.

- If designated as Agent for Executor, the bank assists an individual who has been named as an estate executor and performs many of the administrative tasks, while the Executor retains decision-making responsibilities.

The Customer

The middle-aged, retirement-conscious planner. The investment-conscious, savvy buyer. The close-to-retirement/short-on-savings investor. The very high-net-worth individual concerned about tax liability as well as asset growth and the protection of financial assets. Lawyers, trust officers, accountants, and/or advisors.

Cross Sell:
Estate Settlement Services

↝ Legal Services
To assist with trusts, wills, and certain tax matters

↝ Checking (Current) Account
As a convenient way to keep an accurate record of cash flow

↝ Automatic Teller Machine (ATM)
To access funds at any hour, on any day, at locations worldwide

↝ Portfolio Management
To assist in investment strategies and execution

↝ Mutual Funds
To offer a variety of risk levels and returns for the hands-on investor

↝ Brokerage Services
To buy and sell specific investments with (or without) advice

---

➤ Notes

Contacts	Department	Telephone

Pricing/Fees _____

Miscellaneous _____

Estate Planning Services

This service entails a series of meetings with individuals (and eventually with their attorneys) to determine how and when to pass on their personal assets to the persons they so designate. It can be provided by a wide variety of institutions, from private financial advisors to trust companys, accountants, and lawyers.

Key estate planning objectives require decisions on how to minimize estate taxes, how to distribute family wealth in an orderly fashion, how to simplify the process of settling an estate, and how to reduce administrative expenses in settling an estate.

A typical initial consultation requires that the advisor perform a complete inventory of the estate planner's assets and discuss various estate planning concepts.

Key considerations in planning an estate include the importance of a will, the benefits of establishing a trust, the pros and cons of joint ownership, and the necessity of Durable Power of Attorney and Healthcare Proxy.

After an estate plan has been established, it should be reviewed at least once every five years. Large estates, in particular, should be reviewed annually because of possible changes in the tax laws or the growth of minor children into adults.

The Customer

The middle-aged, retirement-conscious planner. The investment-conscious, savvy buyer. The close-to-retirement/short-on-savings investor. The very high-net-worth individual concerned about tax liability as well as asset growth and the protection of financial assets. Lawyers, trust officers, accountants, and/or advisors.

Cross Sell: Estate Planning Services

➔ Portfolio Management
To assist in investment strategies and execution

➔ Mutual Funds
To offer a variety of risk levels and returns for the hands-on investor

➔ Brokerage Services
To buy and sell specific investments with (or without) advice

➔ Legal Services
To assist with trusts, wills, and certain tax matters

➔ Checking (Current) Account
As a convenient way to keep an accurate record of cash flow

➔ Automatic Teller Machine (ATM)
To access funds at any hour, on any day, at locations worldwide

---

➤ Notes

Contacts	Department	Telephone

Pricing/Fees _____

_____

_____

Miscellaneous _____

_____

_____

Factoring

A financial service for clients interested in selling (or transferring) their accounts receivables to a financial or fiduciary company. This is closely related to the commercial banking concept of "borrowing against receivables," but significantly different in that the factoring company owns the receivables rather than holds the collateral. Factoring naturally involves more risk, and, consequently, a bank will charge more for this service.

The Customer

Most medium-to-large businesses that experience periodic cash-flow problems and seek alternatives to those problems. Banks specifically deal with representatives who can speak knowledgeably about their company's financial condition.

Cross Sell:
Factoring

➙ Business Checking Account
As a prerequisite for any cash management or credit relationship

➙ Line of Credit
To save borrowing time and ensure the availability of funds

➙ Online Balance Reporting
To improve funds management through the monitoring of account balances

➙ Account Analysis
As an easy way to consolidate activity from multiple accounts for better control

➙ Direct Deposit
To have the paychecks of company employees automatically deposited into their accounts

➙ Employee Checking Account
As a convenient, easy way to provide banking services to a company's employees

```
┌─────────────────── Notes ───────────────────┐
│                                              │
│  Contacts         Department      Telephone  │
│  _____  │
│                                              │
│  _____  │
│                                              │
│  _____  │
│                                              │
│  Pricing/Fees_____   │
│                                              │
│  _____  │
│                                              │
│  _____  │
│                                              │
│  Miscellaneous_____   │
│                                              │
│  _____  │
│                                              │
│  _____  │
│                                              │
└──────────────────────────────────────────────┘
```

First-Time Homebuyer

A biweekly mortgage (the payments must be made two times per month) granted only to individuals who have never owned a home or who have had no ownership in the past three years.

This type of mortgage accepts a lower down payment than standard mortgages and the rate is fixed for seven years, then adjusted (one time), then fixed again for the remainder of the mortgage. Another special feature of this mortgage concerns the ratios of annual income to debt, which is expanded in order to allow a first-time homebuyer the opportunity to purchase.

The Customer

As the name of the mortgage implies—someone who has never owned a home before. These customers are usually young (25-35), two-income families, who are stable with children.

Cross Sell:
First-Time Homebuyer

➤ Checking (Current) Account
As a basic account for making monthly payments on the mortgage

➤ Automatic Payment
As an automatic method of making monthly payments without writing checks

➤ Automatic Teller Machine (ATM)
To access funds at any hour, on any day, at locations throughout the world

➤ Direct Deposit
As a safe way to have salary or government checks deposited in a checking account

---

➤ Notes

Contacts	Department	Telephone

Pricing/Fees _____

_____

_____

Miscellaneous _____

_____

_____

Fixed Income and Equity Income Fund

A mutual fund that invests in rather speculative high-yield stock and bonds. This type of fund seeks high current income, and, although it is high risk, in certain economic times these funds can be highly profitable.

The Customer

Speculative investors who don't want to spend the time (or take the chance) buying and selling stocks, bonds, etc.

Cross Sell:
Fixed Income and Equity Income Fund

↦ Deposit Account
(Checking, Money Market or fund with checkbook)
To accept dividends and income and to buy other investments

↦ Margin Account
To buy when the research is convincing, regardless of the deposit account balance

↦ Credit Card
For travel, entertainment, and special purchases

↦ Retirement Account
To accept maximum contributions as defined by law

↦ Trust Services
For expertise in estate planning and investments

▶ Notes

Contacts	Department	Telephone

Pricing/Fees _____

_____

_____

Miscellaneous_____

_____

_____

Fixed-Rate Mortgages

A mortgage in which both the rate and the monthly payments for principal and interest are fixed for the full life of the loan.

The traditional fixed-rate mortgage is thirty years in length; however, mortgages of many different durations are now available to meet diverse customer needs and can be obtained for 7, 10, 15, 20, or 25 years. In addition, many financial institutions offer a biweekly payment option to customers who prefer to make more frequent payments in order to shorten the life of the loan.

Graduated Payment Mortgages (GPM), as well as temporary and permanent buydowns (buydowns reduce the interest rate through the purchase of additional points at the mortgage closing), change the initial payment required by the mortgage note and are available through certain financial institutions.

The Customer

Generally, local individuals planning to reside in their home for many years. Most are two-income families with children.

Cross Sell: Fixed-Rate Mortgages

➛ **Credit Life Insurance**
To pay off the mortgage in the event of the mortgagee's death

➛ **Equity Line of Credit**
As a convenient, tax-advantaged way to make significant purchases

➛ **Checking (Current) Account**
As a convenient way to make mortgage payments directly to the mortgagor

➛ **Automatic Payment**
As an easier and more convenient way than checking to make mortgage payments

➛ **Homeowner's Insurance**
To protect the home against natural or other carefully stipulated disasters

Notes

Contacts Department Telephone

____

____

____

Pricing/Fees ______________________________

____

____

Miscellaneous ______________________________

____

____

Forward Contracts

The buying and selling of foreign currencies. Companies or individuals create a contract between themselves and a bank whereby each agrees to deliver a certain amount of money in one currency in exchange for a certain amount of money in another currency. This transaction must occur at a specified future date and at an agreed-upon rate of exchange.

Forward contracts are done for a couple of reasons. Companies or banks doing business in several countries can maximize their profits for services by being sensitive to foreign exchange rates. Additionally, for many businesses and investors, trading in foreign currencies is simply another investment vehicle, albeit one with a high degree of risk.

The Customer

International businesses buying and selling products and/or services.

Notes

Contacts	Department	Telephone

Pricing/Fees _____

Miscellaneous _____

Cross Sell:
Forward Contracts

→ **International Legal Assistance**
To advise on jurisdictions for minimizing tax liabilities

→ **Foreign Sales Corporation (FSC)**
To provide a more tax-advantaged location for United States exporters

→ **International Business Companies (IBC)**
To provide a more tax-advantaged location for non-United States companies

→ **Business Checking Account**
To provide accurate records of cash flow

→ **Line of Credit**
To save borrowing time and ensure the availability of funds

→ **Online Balance Reporting**
To improve funds management through the monitoring of account balances

→ **Account Analysis**
As an easy way to consolidate activity from multiple accounts for better control

→ **Sweep Investment Account**
To move excess funds to accounts that automatically earn interest

→ **Commercial Loans**
To borrow funds for growth or improvement

→ **Payroll Services**
To reduce the time and cost of processing payroll for employees

Foreign Exchange

This service encompasses two broad definitions. With the first, the service of foreign exchange concerns providing foreign currency to visitors or tourists through consumer banking channels. With the second (and more inclusive) definition, the service involves the trading of foreign currencies through transfers, checks, bills of exchange, and bank notes for the purpose of making a (foreign) payment or settling a "currency exposure risk." The trading aspect of foreign exchange involves buying or selling currencies for the purpose of making gains on rate differentials.

The Customer

Some customers are simply tourists seeking to exchange their currency. Other customers are traders who buy and sell currencies for profit.

Cross Sell: Foreign Exchange

→ **Money Market Account**
To function as a depository

→ **Online Balance Reporting**
To improve fund management through the monitoring of account balances

→ **Computerized Funds Transfer**
To control internal funds transfers through EFT

→ **Credit Card**
To organize travel and related expenses

➤ Notes

Contacts	Department	Telephone

Pricing/Fees _____

_____

_____

Miscellaneous _____

_____

_____

Foreign Sales Corporations (FSC)

The FSC is a legal entity of the United States, that is, a corporation set up to allow the owners of the corporation to benefit from the Tax Reform Act of 1984 (legislation primarily aimed at U.S. exporters). The FSC must maintain an office in a possession or a foreign country that has an acceptable exchange-of-information agreement, such as in the U.S. Virgin Islands, in Barbados, in Bermuda, in the Caymans, in Guam, in Jamaica, or in American Samoa. Many United States citizens use approved FSC locations and companies as addresses and/or accounting centers for business or for personally owned airplanes or yachts.

The Customer

Exporters of the United States, both large and small, seeking to minimize tax liability in their exporting business. These businesspeople are generally well informed by their legal counsel, who recommends (in most cases) the services of the FSC. In this kind of situation, therefore, the primary customer will be an attorney and the secondary customer, the businessperson.

Cross Sell:
Foreign Sales Corporations (FSC)

↪ Checking (Current) Account
To maintain, as required by law, a principal bank account from which the FSC disburses the specific payments

↪ Forward Contracts
To maximize profits through currency trading

↪ Legal and/or Accounting Advice
To handle the intricacies of FSC business

↪ Legal Registration of Yachts, Airplanes
To provide the legal service necessary to operate the craft

↪ Commercial Lending
To borrow for growth or consolidation

➤ Notes

Contacts	Department	Telephone

Pricing/Fees _____

_____

_____

Miscellaneous _____

_____

_____

General Administration of Companies

This service often takes place through a trust company for the purpose of legally establishing a company in a tax friendly environment. In many cases there are no management or production facilities involved in this newly established company; it is simply addressed in a country whose tax laws allow more leniency for another country.

This service includes providing specialized accounting and limited legal services, such as general bookkeeping, preparation of net asset values for offshore mutual funds, portfolio management reports, completion of tax returns, preparation of financial statements, opening bank and brokerage accounts, working with legal counsel, acting as a director, reviewing legal documents, safeguarding share certificates, and communicating with shareholders.

The Customer

High-income, wealthy individuals or offshore companies seeking management and/or administrative assistance from a tax-compatible jurisdiction.

Cross Sell:
General Administration of Companies

↦ Bank Depository Services
To more effectively manage finances

↦ Tax Advice
To stay current with changing tax legislation

↦ Accounting Services
To provide a variety of administrative and bookkeeping services

↦ Forward Contracts
To maximize profits through currency trading

↦ Offshore Mutual Funds
To increase income and/or wealth

↦ Credit Card
To manage travel and related expenses

➤ Notes

Contacts	Department	Telephone

Pricing/Fees _____

_____

_____

Miscellaneous _____

_____

_____

Money Market Fund (General)

A mutual fund that invests in short-term debt securities.

In most cases this type of fund offers a checkbook and is the recipient of dividend payments and sales of stocks or other mutual funds.

A very low-risk investment, the money market fund offers a return only slightly higher than a bank Certificate of Deposit (CD).

The Customer

Investment-conscious individuals who don't want to spend the time (or take the chance) buying and selling stocks, bonds, etc., and who need a depository for investment funds.

Cross Sell:
Money Market Fund (General)

→ Growth and/or Income Mutual Funds
To receive the investment money from the depository

→ Margin Account
To buy when the research is convincing, regardless of the deposit account balance

→ Credit Card
For travel, entertainment, and special purchases

→ Retirement Account
To accept maximum contributions as defined by law

→ Trust Services
For expertise in estate planning and investments

→ Notes

Contacts	Department	Telephone

Pricing/Fees _____

_____

_____

Miscellaneous _____

_____

_____

Growth Fund

A mutual fund that invests in common stocks of established companies. The goal of this type of fund is to achieve high capital gains despite the high risk.

The Customer

Speculative investors who don't want to spend the time buying and selling individual stocks.

Cross Sell:
Growth Fund

→ Deposit Account
(Checking, Money Market or fund with checkbook)
To accept dividends and income and to buy other investments

→ Margin Account
To buy when the research is convincing, regardless of the deposit account balance

→ Credit Card
For travel, entertainment, and special purchases

→ Retirement Account
To accept maximum contributions as defined by law

→ Trust Services
For expertise in estate planning and investments

Notes

Contacts	Department	Telephone

Pricing/Fees _____

_____

_____

Miscellaneous _____

_____

_____

Growth and Income Fund

A mutual fund that invests in companies with solid, proven track records of consistent dividend payments. This type of mutual fund is high-risk, seeking increases in value but mostly increases in current income.

The Customer

Investors who don't want to spend the time (or take the chance) buying and selling individual stocks, bonds, etc., but who nevertheless will tolerate some risk to pursue a better-than-average income.

Cross Sell:
Growth and Income Fund

↳ Deposit Account
(Checking, Money Market or fund with checkbook)
To accept dividends and income and to buy other investments

↳ Margin Account
To buy when the research is convincing, regardless of the deposit account balance

↳ Credit Card
For travel, entertainment, and special purchases

↳ Retirement Account
To accept maximum contributions as defined by law

↳ Trust Services
For expertise in estate planning and investments

→ Notes

Contacts	Department	Telephone

Pricing/Fees _____

_____

_____

Miscellaneous_____

_____

_____

Home Equity Line of Credit

A line of revolving credit based on the equity of a home (approximately 70 percent of the value of the residence minus the remainder of the mortgage, depending on the country). In general, this financial product has no maintenance fees, points, or extra charges and restricts the borrower to certain minimum draws as well as a minimum payment against the line. The interest rate on this product fluctuates depending on the prime rate (in the United States).

An equity line of credit can be used as a cash reserve for major expenditures or emergencies. It has lower interest rates than standard installment loans and, because it is a line of credit, it is much easier to access the funds.

The Customer

Homeowners who need money for major expenditures, such as educations, automobiles, etc.

Cross Sell:
Home Equity Line of Credit

➛ Credit Life Insurance
To pay off the mortgage in the event of the mortgagee's death

➛ First Mortgage Refinancing
As an opportunity for homeowners to assess first mortgages

➛ Checking (Current) Account
As an account into which the disbursed funds of the home equity loan are advanced

➛ Automatic Payment
As an easier and more convenient way than checking to make mortgage payments

➛ Homeowner's Insurance
(Only available through banks in some countries)
To protect the home against natural or other carefully stipulated disasters

---

➤ Notes

Contacts	Department	Telephone

Pricing/Fees _____

Miscellaneous _____

Home Equity Loan

A standard second mortgage in which one lump sum is given to the homeowner, based on the equity in the home. This product is similar to the home equity line of credit, except that the homeowner gets the money all at once and is then required to make set monthly payments for the term of the loan.

In most cases (because this is a second mortgage) there is no appraisal fee, no points, and, depending on the size of the loan, no application fee.

The Customer

Any homeowner who wants to borrow a lump sum of money, repaying a set amount each month.

Cross Sell:
Home Equity Loan

➤ Credit Life Insurance
To pay off the mortgage in the event of the mortgagee's death

➤ First Mortgage Refinancing
As an opportunity for owners to assess their first mortgage

➤ Checking (Current) Account
As an account into which the disbursed funds of the home equity loan are advanced

➤ Automatic Payment
As an easier and more convenient way than checking to make mortgage payments

➤ Homeowner's Insurance
(Only available through banks in some countries)
To protect the home against natural or other carefully stipulated disasters

---

➤ Notes

Contacts	Department	Telephone

Pricing/Fees _____

_____

_____

Miscellaneous _____

_____

_____

Home Improvement Loans

An unsecured loan obtained for the purpose of improving a residence.

These loans are offered to homeowners with terms specifying a set maximum amount that can be borrowed, a determination that is often based on the overall banking relationship between the bank and the borrower. A home improvement loan has a fixed rate, with a 72-month (or sooner) payback.

The Customer

Suburban, family-oriented individuals with growing families, or homeowners who want to improve their property values through renovations, additions, or improvements.

Cross Sell:
Home Improvement Loans

↣ Checking (Current) Account
As a convenient way to keep an accurate record of cash flow

↣ Automatic Teller Machine (ATM)
To access funds at any hour, on any day, at locations worldwide

↣ Direct Deposit
As a safe, reliable way to have paychecks deposited

↣ Mortgage Refinancing
To take advantage of improved mortgage rates

↣ Homeowner's Insurance
(Only available through banks in some countries)
To protect the home against natural and other carefully stipulated disasters

---

→ Notes

Contacts	Department	Telephone

Pricing/Fees _____

_____

_____

Miscellaneous _____

_____

_____

Individually Managed Portfolios

An investment program that a bank manages within the legal investment powers granted by the individual to meet his or her specific financial goals. The extent of investment authority granted is up to the discretion of the customer. In any case, the customer always retains full ownership of assets and the power to terminate the arrangement at any time.

The Customer

Generally middle-aged individuals (with the exception of younger trustees or family financial managers), seeking convenience and no-worry investment plans.

Cross Sell:
Individually Managed Portfolios

→ **Money Market or Checking (Current) Account**
To keep an accurate record of cash flow

→ **Automatic Teller Machine (ATM)**
For access to funds on any day, at any hour, at locations worldwide

→ **Overdraft Protection**
To avoid the inconvenience of an overdraft

→ **Estate Planning**
To assist in overall family financial planning

→ **Tax Advice**
To ensure proper handling of all tax matters

→ Notes

Contacts	Department	Telephone

Pricing/Fees _____

_____

_____

Miscellaneous _____

_____

_____

Individual Retirement Account (IRA)

A retirement product unique to the United States that functions almost like a Certificate of Deposit (CD). The difference between the two is that with an IRA, the customer can put aside tax-deferred retirement dollars ($2,000 individually or $2,250 jointly) and earn higher interest than he or she can with a CD, which is also tax-deferred until age 59 1/2.

The Customer

In many cases, parents who have finished putting their children through college and are now concerned about retirement. In addition, many younger individuals who are concerned about their eventual retirement income and the possible inadequacy of the United States social security system to provide for their future needs.

Cross Sell:
Individual Retirement Account (IRA)

➞ Checking (Current) Account
To keep an accurate record of cash flow

➞ Automatic Teller Machine (ATM)
For cash at any hour, on any day, at locations worldwide

➞ Savings Account
To save money for IRAs and to link it with checking

➞ Overdraft Protection
To avoid the inconvenience of an accidental overdraft

➞ Estate Planning
To assist in overall family financial planning

➞ Notes

Contacts	Department	Telephone

Pricing/Fees _____

Miscellaneous _____

International Business Companies (IBC)

These companies are similar to FSCs; however, IBCs are for non-United States companies. IBCs provide a variety of services for companies, including management and administration of funds at an offshore location.

The Customer

High-income, wealthy individuals or an offshore company seeking management and/or administrative assistance from a tax-compatible jurisdiction.

Cross Sell:
International Business Companies (IBC)

➜ Bank Depository Services
To more effectively manage finances

➜ Tax Advice
To stay current with changing tax legislation

➜ Accounting Services
To provide a variety of administrative and bookkeeping services

➜ Forward Contracts
To maximize profits through currency trading

➜ Offshore Mutual Funds
To increase income and/or wealth

➜ Credit Card
To manage travel and related expenses

➤ Notes

Contacts	Department	Telephone

Pricing/Fees _____

_____

_____

Miscellaneous_____

_____

_____

International Fund Administration

This service is provided by trust companies (or specialized accounting technology companies) with major investments in computer technology, accounting, and investment services. It involves providing full accounting (up to and including calculating daily net-asset values) and limited legal services to mutual funds (primarily offshore or international funds).

The Customer

Fund and/or money market managers and administrative staff of mutual funds.

Cross Sell:
International Fund Administration

➤ International Business Corporations (IBC)
To control tax vulnerability

➤ Checking or Money Market Depository
As the source for funds availability

➤ Online Balance Reporting
To improve funds management through the monitoring of account balances and of transaction history

➤ Account Analysis
To consolidate activity from multiple accounts

➤ Forward Contracts
To maximize profits through currency trading

➤ Ongoing Legal Services
To advise on tax and jurisdictional matters

➤ Notes

Contacts	Department	Telephone

Pricing/Fees _____

Miscellaneous_____

International Letter of Credit

An agreement by a United States bank to pay for the purchase of goods by one of its customers according to specific terms. These letters are most commonly used by business people who import goods from overseas. Standard terms require the bank to pay the beneficiary (usually the exporter) after the goods have been shipped and by the expiration date of the letter of credit. Documentation of the scheduled shipment must be examined by the bank prior to the bank's release of funds to the beneficiary. By issuing a letter of credit, the bank is, in fact, substituting its creditworthiness for that of its customer, thus assuring payment to the exporter for the goods being shipped.

Determining a borrower's creditworthiness is the bank's first step when asked to provide a letter of credit. The bank loan officer must establish that the borrower has sufficient funds to pay for the goods according to the letter's terms. The kind of documentation required of a borrower on a letter of credit is generally the same as it is for any commercial loan. The fee is often a percentage of the amount guaranteed in the letter.

The Customer

Financial officer of a company that specializes (in most cases) in international dealings.

Cross Sell: International Letter of Credit

➛ **Checking or Money Market Depository**
As the source for funds availability

➛ **Online Balance Reporting**
To improve funds management through the monitoring of account balances and of transaction history

➛ **Account Analysis**
To consolidate activity from multiple accounts

➛ **Forward Contracts**
To maximize profits through currency trading

➛ **Ongoing Legal Services**
To advise on tax and jurisdictional matters

Notes

Contacts	Department	Telephone

Pricing/Fees ____________________

____

____

Miscellaneous ____________________

____

____

Investment Management

An investment program that the financial institution manages within the investment powers granted to it by the customer. The customer, however, retains full ownership of his or her assets and the power to terminate the arrangement at any time.

Investment management is sometimes referred to as portfolio management, and is offered as a trust service.

The Customer

Anyone who has accumulated some assets and either isn't interested in managing those assets or doesn't feel comfortable doing it.

Cross Sell:
Investment Management

➤ Estate Planning
To assist in overall family financial planning

➤ Brokerage Services
To buy and sell specific investments with (or without) advice

➤ Mutual Funds
To offer a variety of risk levels and returns for the hands-on investor

➤ Legal Services
To assist with trusts, wills, and certain tax matters

➤ Sweep Account
To maximize interest income

➤ Business (or Personal) Money Market Account
As an interest-earning alternative to standard checking and a convenient way to keep an accurate record of cash flow

➤ Automatic Teller Machine (ATM)
To access funds at any hour, on any day, at locations worldwide

➤ Home Equity Line of Credit
As a convenient way to have tax-advantaged funds available for a variety of purposes

---

➤ Notes

Contacts	Department	Telephone

Pricing/Fees _____

Miscellaneous _____

Individual Retirement Account (IRA) Savings

A U.S. savings/retirement product that accumulates invested monies and can be rolled over at the appropriate time into an IRA Certificate of Deposit (CD) or into an investment account.

With this investment vehicle, the owner can make either regularly scheduled direct deposits or periodic investments. Monthly statements list all principal and interest, all or part of which can be rolled into an IRA investment account on customer's instruction. The interest on IRA savings is instantly tax-deferred.

The Customer

Conscientious saver, planning for retirement.

Cross Sell:
Individual Retirement Account (IRA) Savings

→ Home Equity Credit Line
As an easy source for providing maximum funding for an IRA

→ Personal Loan
As an alternative source for funding an IRA

→ Certificate of Deposit (CD)
As a safe, secure investment

→ Checking (Current) Account
As a convenient, accurate way to control cash flow

→ Estate Planning
To assist in overall family financial planning

➤ Notes

Contacts	Department	Telephone

Pricing/Fees _____

_____

_____

Miscellaneous _____

_____

_____

Internal Revenue Service (IRS) Reporting Service

An electronic or magnetic filing of W2 or 1099 standard Internal Revenue Service forms. The bank filing of these forms is offered to the customer in two ways:

- Full filing includes electronic transmission to the IRS and the printing of the forms.
- Partial filing does not include printing of forms.

The fee for this service is based on the number of W2 or 1099 forms that the bank fills out.

The Customer

Business owner or financial officer, bookkeeper, tax specialist.

Cross Sell:
Internal Revenue Service (IRS) Reporting Service

→ **Electronic Banking Interface**
To control funds transfers through Automated Clearing House (ACH)

→ **Employee Benefit Services**
To provide added value in employee/employer relations

→ **Credit Line**
To borrow on an as-needed basis

→ **Accounting and Tax Advice**
To validate financial decisions

→ Notes

Contacts	Department	Telephone

Pricing/Fees _____

_____

_____

Miscellaneous_____

_____

_____

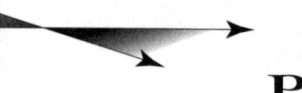

Keogh Plans

U.S. profit-sharing and money-purchase plans for self-employed individuals who desire a retirement program.

A business owner (self-employed individual) can contribute tax-deferred income annually (up to 25 percent of covered compensation or up to $30,000 per employee). The annual contributions under a defined benefit Keogh Plan vary, depending on an employee's length of service with the company, the amount of an employee's salary, and the availability of funds within the company.

Many banks handle the administrative duties associated with these plans and file the appropriate IRS forms on behalf of self-employed individuals.

Business owners must contribute on behalf of their full-time employees if they contribute for themselves. Contributions for any given tax year may be made up to the tax-filing deadline of the following year, including extensions.

The Customer

Businesses and their employees.

Cross Sell: Keogh Plans

→ Home Equity Credit Line
As an easy source for providing maximum funding for a Keogh

→ Personal Loan
As an alternative source for funding a Keogh

→ Certificate of Deposit (CD)
As a safe, secure investment

→ Checking (Current) Account
As a convenient, accurate way to control cash flow

→ Estate Planning
To assist in overall family financial planning

➤ Notes

Contacts	Department	Telephone

Pricing/Fees _____

_____

_____

Miscellaneous _____

_____

_____

Land Loan

A real estate loan that, although granted for acquiring land on which a house or other family property can be built, does not have to be used for the specific purpose of building.

Most banks have a fairly standard, straightforward policy toward land loans. First, the property to be bought must be properly zoned according to local ordinances with regard to the number of family units and type of occupancy. Second, the amount of the loan should not exceed 70 percent of the sales price or appraised value of the land (loan-to-value percentage = 70%).

These loans must be repaid within ten years and cannot be converted to a mortgage.

The Customer

A developer or builder, or even an individual who is just buying land as an investment.

Cross Sell:
Land Loan

→ **Checking (Current) Account**
To pay the installments

→ **Automatic Payment**
To ensure that the payments are made on time

→ **Construction Loan**
As an option when and if the owner decides to build

→ **Mortgage**
To finance the home

➤ **Notes**

Contacts	Department	Telephone

Pricing/Fees _____

_____

_____

Miscellaneous _____

_____

_____

Late Deposit Window

Late deposits of large, daily sums are delivered directly to a bank's operations center, thereby significantly reducing float time as well as increasing the availability of funds in commercial accounts. Commercial customers make prior arrangements for late deposits with a stipulated bank department or a branch.

The Customer

Business owner or financial officer of a company.

Cross Sell:
Late Deposit Window

→ Online Balance Reporting
To improve account management through monitoring balances and transaction history

→ Sweep Investment Account
To sweep excess funds to accounts that earn higher interest

→ Commercial Loan
To achieve profits through carefully advised lending

→ Line of Credit
To access funds on an as-needed basis

Notes

Contacts	Department	Telephone

Pricing/Fees _____

Miscellaneous _____

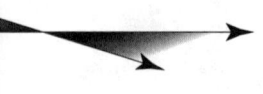

Life Insurance

Insurance on an individual's life expectancy. (See Savings Bank Life Insurance [SBLI]). There are varieties of life insurance available through life insurance companies, as well as through many banks and financial institutions. These policies, which are based on an individual's specific investment or insurance needs, can be purchased in the forms of whole life, term life, or universal life.

The Customer

Individuals seeking a variety of vehicles that will provide an element of security to their lifestyles and to those who are dependent on them.

Notes

Contacts	Department	Telephone

Pricing/Fees _____

_____

_____

Miscellaneous _____

_____

_____

Cross Sell:
Life Insurance

➤ Estate Planning
To assist in overall family financial planning

➤ Annuities
As tax-advantaged methods of withdrawing funds for retirement

➤ Brokerage Services
To buy and sell specific investments with (or without) advice

➤ Homeowner's Insurance
(Only available through banks in some countries) To protect the home against natural and other carefully stipulated disasters

➤ Legal Services
To assist with trusts, wills, and certain tax matters

➤ Sweep Investment Account
To maximize interest income

➤ Money Market Account
As an alternative to standard checking—earns interest and is a convenient way to keep an accurate record of cash flow

➤ Automatic Teller Machine (ATM)
To access funds at any hour, on any day, at locations worldwide

➤ Home Equity Line of Credit
As a convenient way to have tax-advantaged funds available for a variety of purposes

Life Insurance Trust

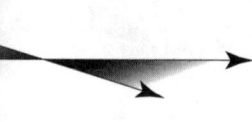

A trust that is set up to distribute the proceeds of an individual's life insurance policy, free from interference of probate.

When the individual who sets up this trust (the grantor) dies, the bank (as trustee) collects the proceeds, invests them prudently, and distributes income to the beneficiaries according to the grantor's instructions. Life insurance trusts assure grantors that the proceeds of their policies will be professionally managed, invested, and distributed according to the stated objectives and needs of the grantor.

This type of trust usually offers more options for distributing proceeds than most life insurance policies. By irrevocably passing ownership of life insurance policies to this trust, an individual can be assured that estate taxes can be avoided. To qualify for savings in estate taxes, ownership of life insurance policies must be passed irrevocably to a trust at least three years before the death of the grantor.

The Customer

Individuals seeking a variety of vehicles that will provide an element of security to their lifestyles and to their dependents.

Cross Sell:
Life Insurance Trust

→ Estate Planning
To assist in overall family financial planning

→ Annuities
As tax-advantaged methods of withdrawing funds for retirement

→ Brokerage Services
To buy and sell specific investments with (or without) advice

→ Homeowner's Insurance
(Only available through banks in some countries) To protect the home against natural and other carefully stipulated disasters

→ Legal Services
To assist with trusts, wills, and certain tax matters

→ Money Market Account
As an alternative to standard checking—earns interest and is a convenient way to keep an accurate record of cash flow

→ Automatic Teller Machine (ATM)
To access funds at any hour, on any day, at locations worldwide

---

→ Notes

Contacts	Department	Telephone

Pricing/Fees _____

Miscellaneous _____

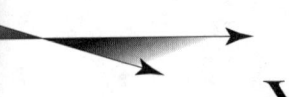

Mastercard/Visa

A retail credit card for consumer purchases. To obtain one, prospective credit card users can make an application at most banks, at retail stores, or through "800" numbers. Applicants can choose among cards that feature an endless range of incentives, for example: multiple cards at no additional cost; no annual fee for the first year; choice of fixed- or variable-rate accounts; cash advances charged at 2 percent of the cash advance amount; year-end summary of charges.

Mastercard and Visa are accepted at over eight million locations worldwide, and most offer extended warranty protection on credit card purchases. Additionally, if the balances are paid in full each month, the credit card holder eliminates accrued interest charges. Liberal credit lines assure cardholders that personal credit is readily available when needed.

For the traveler, it is possible to choose a credit card that offers free travel accident insurance for the family, free lost luggage protection up to $3,000, free collision deductible insurance for rental cars up to $15,000, and free credit card registration and purchase protection (for most items).

The Customer

In today's credit-oriented world, almost anyone is a customer for a credit card.

Cross Sell: Mastercard/Visa

→ **Checking (Current) Account**
As a service compatible with the bank's credit card

→ **Automatic Teller Machine (ATM)**
To access funds at any hour, on any day, at locations worldwide

→ **Overdraft Protection**
As a cost-saving measure in the event of an accidental overdraft

→ **Savings Account**
As a link to checking via the ATM card

Notes

Contacts	Department	Telephone

Pricing/Fees _____

_____

_____

Miscellaneous _____

_____

_____

Merchant Banking

This is a commercial banking function in which a merchant banker seeks venture capital or partnerships from businesses (and high-net-worth individuals) for the purpose of capital market transactions, mergers, and takeovers. With this service, the banker also might assist corporate finance clients, guide company restructuring (by virtue of providing the capital), and handle leveraged buyouts. Although some merchant bankers provide risk capital, most prefer to coordinate the capital and perhaps take a small position (depending on the perceived risk).

The Customer

Other merchant bankers, financial institutions, high-net-worth individuals and their advisors, lawyers, etc.

Cross Sell: Merchant Banking

→ **Commercial Loan**
To increase investment power

→ **Brokerage Services**
To shift equity holdings into other speculative ventures

→ **Tax Advice**
To stay current with changing tax legislation

→ **Accounting Services**
To provide a variety of administrative and bookkeeping services

→ **Offshore Mutual Funds**
To increase income and/or wealth

→ **Business and Personal Depository (Checking Current Account)**
A convenient way to keep an accurate record of cash flow

→ **Credit Card**
To manage travel and related expenses

→ **Trust Services**
To offer proven experts in the area of investments and planning

→ **Legal Services**
To assist with trusts, wills, and certain tax matters

→ Notes

Contacts	Department	Telephone

Pricing/Fees _____

_____

Miscellaneous _____

_____

Money Market Account

A checking account that earns money-market interest rates that are often tiered to specific deposit levels. Interest is compounded monthly and credited at the end of each statement cycle. These accounts require a higher minimum balance than NOW accounts and therefore offer limited check-writing and limited automatic withdrawals. Direct deposit (electronic transfer of funds) allows customers to make deposits without visiting the bank branch.

This account should be used for savings and for writing occasional checks.

The Customer

Average customers, employed, needing some financial management in their lives.

Cross Sell:
Money Market Account

➤ Checking (Current) Account
As a convenient way to pay bills and keep an accurate record of cash flow

➤ Automatic Teller Machine (ATM)
To access funds at any hour, on any day, at locations worldwide

➤ Direct Deposit
As a safe, quick way to have paychecks deposited

➤ Overdraft Protection
To spare customers the embarrassment of accidental overdraft

➤ Statement Savings
To link checking to savings to money market via the ATM card

➤ Equity Credit Line
As a quick method of having extra money for many purchases in a tax-advantaged way

---

➤ Notes

Contacts	Department	Telephone

Pricing/Fees _____

_____

_____

Miscellaneous _____

_____

Money Market Fund (General)

A mutual fund that invests in short-term-debt securities.

In most cases this type of fund offers a checkbook and is the recipient of dividend payments and sales of stocks or other mutual funds.

A very low-risk investment, the money market fund offers a return only slightly higher than a bank Certificate of Deposit (CD).

The Customer

Investment-conscious individuals who don't want to spend the time (or take the chance) buying and selling stocks, bonds, etc., and who need a depository for investment funds.

Cross Sell:
Money Market Fund (General)

➤ Growth and/or Income Mutual Funds
To receive the investment money from the depository

➤ Margin Account
To buy when the research is convincing, regardless of the deposit account balance

➤ Credit Card
For travel, entertainment, and special purchases

➤ Retirement Account
To accept maximum contributions as defined by law

➤ Trust Services
For expertise in estate planning and investments

➤ Notes

Contacts	Department	Telephone

Pricing/Fees _____

Miscellaneous _____

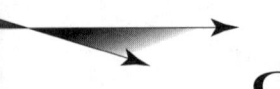

Money Order

An instrument in the form of a check purchased by customers who are paying "cash" or money order demands. A money order, though in check form, is universally accepted as cash and therefore cannot bounce.

When a money order is purchased, the names of both the purchaser and the payee appear on the check.

Most banks will not charge for a money order if the Customer has an account with the bank; otherwise there is a nominal charge.

The Customer

Frequently, a customer without a checking account who must make a non-cash payment. In other instances, a customer who is fulfilling a "cash only" request of a vendor.

Cross Sell:
Money Order

➔ Checking (Current) Account
As a convenient way to pay bills and keep an accurate record of cash flow

➔ Automatic Teller Machine (ATM)
To access funds at any hour, on any day, at locations worldwide

➔ Direct Deposit
As a safe way to have paychecks deposited without having to visit the bank

➔ Savings Account
To link to the checking account via the ATM card

➔ Notes

Contacts	Department	Telephone

Pricing/Fees _____

_____

_____

Miscellaneous _____

_____

_____

Municipal Bond Fund

A mutual fund that invests in bonds exempt from state, local, and federal taxes. This type of fund is one of moderate risk, seeking tax-free income.

In many cases a municipal bond fund offers a checkbook and is the recipient of dividend payments and sales of stocks or other mutual funds.

The Customer

Investment-conscious individuals who don't want to spend the time (or take the chance) buying and selling individual bonds and who need a depository for investment funds.

Cross Sell:
Municipal Bond Fund

→ Deposit Account
(Checking, money market or fund with checkbook) To accept dividends and income and to buy other investments

→ Growth and/or Income Mutual Funds
To receive investment money from the depository

→ Brokerage Services (or Discount Brokerage)
For investment in researched equities

→ Margin Account
To buy when the research is convincing, regardless of the deposit account balance

→ Credit Card
For travel, entertainment, and special purchases

→ Retirement Account
To accept maximum contributions as defined by law

→ Trust Services
For expertise in estate planning and investments

→ Estate Planning
To assist in overall family financial planning

→ Notes

Contacts	Department	Telephone

Pricing/Fees _____

_____

_____

Miscellaneous _____

_____

Municipal Department

A department of a bank that serves many of the financial needs of the cities, towns, school districts, housing authorities, and hospitals located in the bank's marketplace. These institutions primarily use the bank's depository services, such as business checking accounts, municipal money market accounts, and selected cash management products.

A bank's municipal department makes the following short-term borrowing programs available to municipal customers:

- Bond Anticipation Note. The bank loans funds with the understanding that the note will be repaid shortly with proceeds from issuance of bonds.

- Tax Anticipation Note. Similar to the above, except that this type of note is repaid from collected property taxes.

In some cases, municipalities and other governmental agencies can arrange for long-term borrowing (one year or longer).

Notes

Contacts　　　　　Department　　　　　Telephone

_____

_____

_____

Pricing/Fees _____

_____

_____

Miscellaneous_____

_____

_____

Mutual Funds

A collection of stocks, bonds, or other securities purchased by a group of investors and managed by a professional investment company.

A range of mutual fund portfolios are often offered by retail and commercial banks. These funds are designed to meet the financial objectives of investors, and they also "factor in" each individual investor's tolerance for risk. Regulations governing the selling of mutual funds require banks in the United States to offer personal consultation with investors in order to assess their financial position and to determine the portfolio that best suits their needs. When banks offer this type of service, the mutual fund portfolios normally are made up of a diversity of no-load mutual funds, freeing investors from paying up-front fees. These portfolios are highly liquid, easily redeemable, and can be adjusted to meet changes in financial needs.

Major categories of mutual funds are: Aggressive Growth Funds, Growth Funds, Growth and Income Funds, Fixed Income and Equity Income Funds, Option Income Funds, General Money Market Funds, U.S. Government Money Market Funds, Balanced Funds, Tax-Free Money Market Funds, and Municipal Bond Funds. In addition, there are Offshore Mutual Funds, which are available worldwide except to citizens of the United States.

Brief descriptions of these funds are included alphabetically in this guide.

The Customer

Investors who don't want to spend the time (or take the chance) buying and selling stocks, bonds, etc.

Cross Sell: Mutual Funds

➔ Deposit Account
(Checking, money market or fund with checkbook) To accept dividends and income and to buy other investments

➔ Margin Account
To buy when the research is convincing, regardless of the deposit account balance

➔ Credit Card
For travel, entertainment, and special purchases

➔ Retirement Account
To accept maximum contributions as defined by law

➔ Trust Services
For expertise in estate planning and investments

➔ Estate Planning
To assist in overall family financial planning

Notes

Contacts	Department	Telephone

Pricing/Fees _____

_____

_____

Miscellaneous_____

_____

_____

Night Depository Bags

Deposit bags that the bank furnishes to depositors and businesses who need to deposit their daily cash and other receipts after normal banking hours.

With this service, a business rents both a deposit bag and keys for as long as it expects to make after-hours deposits. Money within the bag is counted and deposited into the depositor's account the next morning. Businesses who daily handle large amounts of cash and receipts depend on this service for a couple of reasons. By using night depository bags, for example, businesses can feel secure knowing that their deposits are safely stored for the night. Additionally, businesses need not interrupt the workday to ensure the deposit is made promptly.

Banks commonly charge an annual fee for the bag and for the keys.

The Customer

A retail business dealing in cash.

Cross Sell:
Night Depository Bags

→ Line of Credit
To save borrowing time and ensure the availability of funds

→ Direct Deposit
To have employees' paychecks automatically deposited into their accounts

→ Statement Savings
As an interest-bearing savings for funds

→ Commercial Loan
To borrow for growth, debt consolidation, etc.

▶ Notes

Contacts	Department	Telephone

Pricing/Fees _____

_____

_____

Miscellaneous_____

_____

_____

Notary Public

A person commissioned to act as a "state" for a specific period of time, and, as such, is empowered to administer certain oaths as well as to attest to and to certify documents. A notary public can also protest negotiable instruments for nonpayment or nonacceptance.

The Customer

Anyone needing documents notarized.

Cross Sell:
Notary Public

➝ Checking (Current) Account
As a convenient way to pay bills and keep an accurate record of cash flow

➝ Automatic Teller Machine (ATM)
To access funds at any hour, on any day, at locations worldwide

➝ Direct Deposit
As a safe way to have paychecks deposited without going to the bank

➝ Savings Account
To link to the checking account via the ATM card

➤ Notes

Contacts	Department	Telephone

Pricing/Fees _____

_____

_____

Miscellaneous _____

_____

_____

NOW Account

A NOW (Notice of Withdrawal) Account is actually a type of savings account that issues checks, pays interest on unused balances, and accepts direct deposits and automatic withdrawals, such as insurance premium payments. These accounts were first used around the early '70s in the New England area of the United States. They require specified minimum daily balances in order to avoid monthly maintenance fees. Interest on NOW accounts, which compounds monthly on balances of any level, is credited at the end of each statement period.

The Customer

Average customers, employed, needing some financial management in their lives.

Cross Sell: NOW Account

→ Automatic Teller Machine (ATM)
To access funds at any hour, on any day, at locations worldwide

→ Direct Deposit
As a safe, quick way to have paychecks deposited

→ Overdraft Protection
To spare customers the embarrassment of accidental overdraft

→ Statement Savings
To link checking to savings via the ATM card

→ Equity Credit Line
As a quick method of having extra money for purchases in a tax-advantaged way

---

Notes

Contacts	Department	Telephone

Pricing/Fees _____

Miscellaneous _____

Online Balance Reporting

Direct, online access to account balance and activity information through the use of a personal computer. Account information shows not only the current statement period but also the previous period.

Users of this service can call up several different screens that show information on account balances, float balances, hold amounts, and selected credits and debits.

To print these screens, producing what is commonly referred to as "hard copy," all one needs is a computer printer.

Online balance reporting is a service for which the customer is charged a one-time installation fee, a monthly service fee, and a monthly fee for each additional account.

The Customer

Business owner, or a financial officer of a business.

Cross Sell:
Online Balance Reporting

→ Computerized Funds Transfer
To control funds transfers internally through Automated Clearing House (ACH)

→ Asset-Based Lending
As a way to borrow money against inventory

→ Credit Card
To control travel and entertainment expenses

→ Payroll Services
To reduce the time and cost of processing payroll for employees

→ Notes

Contacts	Department	Telephone

Pricing/Fees _____

_____

_____

Miscellaneous _____

_____

_____

Option Income Fund

A mutual fund that invests in dividend-paying common stock on which call options are traded.

This type of fund is high-risk, seeking high current income.

The Customer

Speculative investors who don't want to spend the time (or take the chance) buying and selling stocks, bonds, etc.

Cross Sell:
Option Income Fund

→ **Deposit Account**
(Checking, money market or fund with checkbook) To accept dividends and income and to buy other investments

→ **Margin Account**
To buy when the research is convincing, regardless of the deposit account balance

→ **Credit Card**
For travel, entertainment, and special purchases

→ **Retirement Account**
To accept maximum contributions as defined by law

→ **Trust Services**
For expertise in estate planning and investments

Notes

Contacts	Department	Telephone

Pricing/Fees _____

Miscellaneous _____

Overdraft Protection

A personal line of credit attached to a customer's checking account. Funds are advanced in stipulated increments up to the available credit limit to cover an overdraft. The fee is an adjustable interest rate based on the prime rate.

This service enables banking customers to avoid overdraft charges, as well as the embarrassment of a bounced check. Additionally, overdraft protection guards against the kind of bad credit that results from sloppy bookkeeping.

The Customer

Those who spend close to (or in excess of) their account balances would benefit from this kind of backup. Many banks automatically offer this service to creditworthy customers who hold checking accounts with them.

Cross Sell:
Overdraft Protection

→ Checking (Current) Account
As necessary for overdraft protection

→ Direct Deposit
As a safe, reliable way to have paychecks deposited

→ Automatic Teller Machine (ATM)
To access funds at any hour, on any day, at locations worldwide

→ Home Equity Line of Credit
As a convenient way to have tax-advantaged funds available for a variety of purposes

---

Notes

Contacts	Department	Telephone

Pricing/Fees _____

_____

_____

Miscellaneous _____

_____

_____

Passbook Loans

A secured loan in which the bank holds a customer's passbook or Certificate of Deposit (CD) as collateral.

These are very common loans that allow customers to borrow a maximum amount of 95 percent of balance against their collateralized account. The rates for these loans are fixed, with an expected payback in one year.

The reason for the popularity of the passbook loan is its easy application process: there is no waiting for approval, the funds are available immediately, and there is no need to withdraw savings for unexpected cash needs.

The Customer

Customers with passbook savings accounts who need an instant loan for a short period of time—a year or less.

Cross Sell:
Passbook Loans

↪ Passbook Savings
As a prerequisite for the loan

↪ Checking (Current) Account
As a convenient way to keep an accurate record of cash flow

↪ Automatic Teller Machine (ATM)
To access funds at any hour, on any day, at locations worldwide

↪ Direct Deposit
As a safe, reliable way to have paychecks deposited

➤ Notes

Contacts	Department	Telephone

Pricing/Fees _____

_____

_____

Miscellaneous_____

_____

_____

Passbook Savings

When banks first considered offering savings accounts to their customers, they did so in the form of passbook savings —a plainly formatted accounting of a customer's savings activity, recorded, by hand, in the bank.

The original procedure for passbook savings was simple—customers deposited money into their financial institution and received, in return, a small book that listed, by date, such account activity as deposits, withdrawals, and bank fees. To attract depositors and to compensate them for their funds, the bank paid interest on the balance (either daily or monthly) and sometimes even paid varying interest, depending on the amount of money kept in the account.

Changes in banking technology have rendered obsolete many of the early features of passbook savings. Most passbook accounts today, for example, require a minimum balance, which exempts the customer from incurring a monthly maintenance fee. In addition, although customers still receive a passbook, banks issue them solely for the customer's personal record keeping, as quarterly statements are now used to itemize the customer's savings activity.

This account is ideal for customers who want to have a savings record available at all times. Because interest rates for this kind of savings account are so low, most customers use it for short-term savings, transferring funds to higher-interest investments when enough money has been saved.

The Customer

Many senior citizens still use this type of account, as do others who feel the need of having a record of savings available to them at all times.

Cross Sell:
Passbook Savings

➔ Certificate of Deposit (CD)
As a safe, conservative investment with higher returns than with passbook savings

➔ Direct Deposit
As a safe, quick way of having social security (or other paychecks) deposited into a banking account

➔ Safe Deposit Box
As a convenient, secure place for valuables

Notes

Contacts	Department	Telephone

Pricing/Fees _____

_____

_____

Miscellaneous _____

_____

_____

Payroll Bonds Processing

An employer-implemented purchase of Series EE bonds for employees through payroll deductions. The bank electronically orders bonds in any denomination and then mails them either to the employer or directly to employees. A computerized system tracks payroll purchase schedules and handles accruing amounts from each payday or full cash deductions.

There is often no charge for this service; however, a business checking account is frequently required.

The Customer

A business owner or financial officer of a company.

Cross Sell: Payroll Bonds Processing

➔ Sweep Investment Account
To sweep excess funds to higher-interest accounts

➔ Employee Benefits
As retirement and profit sharing programs for employees and owners

➔ Certificates of Deposit (CD)
As an FDIC-insured investment with a fixed rate of interest

➔ Payroll Services
To reduce the time and cost of processing payroll for employees

---

➔ Notes

Contacts	Department	Telephone

Pricing/Fees _____

_____

_____

Miscellaneous_____

_____

_____

Pension Fund

A broad range of products and services comprise the category of pension funds. Many customers refer to all of them interchangeably (Also referred to as Profit Sharing Plan, IRA, 401(k), or Retirement Plan).

A pension fund is a savings fund that is put aside for an individual's retirement. Most of these funds are tax-advantaged, meaning that the money (and interest earned on that money) is free (or mostly free) from taxes until a stipulated age is reached (59 1/2 in the United States). The individual may contribute specified amounts to the fund, depending on the salary of the individual.

Usually both employer and employee participate in company-sponsored pension funds, with the employer frequently matching an employee's contribution with stock (a stock-option program) or some other kind of financial product. (See Simplified Employee Pension [SEP] and Keogh.)

The Customer

Primarily customers over forty, usually about the age most people begin to think seriously about retirement. Bankers and trust officers in the United States are likely to encounter both men and women with Individual Retirement Accounts (IRAs) or some kind of a 401(k) plan, either of which the customer has been funding (or is about to become serious about funding). Customers range from those with average to above-average income, anywhere from $40k to $200k. Children. Homeowner. Two cars.

Cross Sell:
Pension Fund

⇢ Estate Planning
To assist in overall family financial planning

⇢ Annuities
As tax-advantaged methods of withdrawing funds for retirement

⇢ Money Market Account
As an alternative to standard checking—earns interest, and is a convenient way to keep an accurate record of cash flow

⇢ Automatic Teller Machine (ATM)
To access funds at any hour, on any day, at locations worldwide

⇢ Brokerage Services
To buy and sell specific investments with (or without) advice

⇢ Homeowners Insurance
(Only available through banks in some countries) to protect the home against natural and other carefully stipulated disasters

⇢ Legal Services
To assist with trusts, wills, and certain tax matters

➤ Notes

Contacts	Department	Telephone

Pricing/Fees _____

Miscellaneous _____

Permanent Construction Loans

A new-home financing package that consists of a construction loan to finance the building of a residential structure, and which is later converted into a permanent mortgage with a term of up to thirty years, after construction is completed. Only one legal closing is necessary for this type of loan.

The maximum amount of this loan generally cannot exceed 90 percent of the appraised value of the land and completed structure.

The borrower must complete construction within an agreed-upon period in order to convert the construction loan to a permanent mortgage and must request an approved underwriter to arrange an inspection of a completed home.

The Customer

A developer or builder, or even a nonprofessional who is simply buying land as an investment.

Cross Sell:
Permanent Construction Loans

➛ Checking (Current) Account
To pay the installments

➛ Automatic Payment
To ensure that payments are made on time

➛ Construction Loan
As an option when or if the owner decides to build

➛ Mortgage
To finance the home

➤ Notes

Contacts	Department	Telephone

Pricing/Fees _____

_____

_____

Miscellaneous_____

_____

_____

Personal Line of Credit

A personal line of credit is an unsecured loan available to creditworthy customers of a bank. This account allows customers to authorize the bank to make a deposit into their personal deposit account whenever they request it. A simple phone call to the bank releases the requested funds, which are then immediately deposited in the account, allowing for instant access.

A personal line of credit does have a minimum draw with minimum increments, and is subject to an adjustable interest rate determined by the bank.

The Customer

Creditworthy individuals who are familiar with banking services and who might be spending close to (or in excess of) their limit.

Cross Sell:
Personal Line of Credit

➻ Checking (Current) Account
As a prerequisite for any line of credit

➻ Direct Deposit
As a safe, reliable way to have paychecks deposited

➻ Automatic Teller Machine (ATM)
To access funds at any hour, on any day, at locations worldwide

➻ Home Equity Line of Credit
As a convenient way to have tax-advantaged funds available for a variety of purposes

---

➤ Notes

Contacts	Department	Telephone

Pricing/Fees _____

_____

_____

Miscellaneous _____

_____

_____

Personal Trust Services

A legal arrangement in which individuals authorize a bank, as their trustee or co-trustee, to hold and manage property transferred to a trust for the benefit of another person or persons.

Personal trust services typically are set up to save on estate taxes and to provide ongoing asset management for families after the death of the grantor. As trustee, the bank invests assets, distributes income and/or principal to beneficiaries, makes tax decisions, issues account statements, and files the trust's tax returns.

The Customer

The middle-aged, retirement-conscious planner. The investment-conscious, savvy buyer. The close-to-retirement/short-on-savings investor. The very high-net-worth individual concerned about tax liability as well as asset growth and the protection of financial assets. Lawyers, trust officers, accountants, and/or advisors.

Cross Sell:
Personal Trust Service

→ **Estate Planning**
To assist in overall family financial planning

→ **Portfolio Management**
To assist in investment strategies and execution

→ **Mutual Funds**
To offer a variety of risk levels and returns for the hands-on investor

→ **Brokerage Services**
To buy and sell specific investments with (or without) advice

→ **Legal Services**
To assist with trusts, wills, and certain tax matters

→ **Checking (Current) Account**
As a convenient way to keep an accurate record of cash flow

→ **Automatic Teller Machine (ATM)**
To access funds at any hour, on any day, at locations worldwide

→ **Home Equity Line of Credit**
As a convenient way to have tax-advantaged funds available for a variety of purposes

---

→ Notes

Contacts	Department	Telephone

Pricing/Fees _____

Miscellaneous _____

Portfolio Management

The analysis and management of a portfolio of investments belonging to an individual, corporation, or institution.

The financial institution works with investors to identify their needs and financial goals and to determine the appropriate mix of investments that will make up the portfolio.

With individually managed portfolios, individuals with substantial assets are relieved of the need to keep up with investment alternatives, market conditions, and financial research responsibilities related to the time-sensitive buying or selling of investments.

The customer has final say on every decision-making aspect of the management of the portfolio, from investment objectives to deposits/withdrawal of income generated by the investments.

The Customer

The financially successful, middle-aged, retirement-conscious planner. The very high-net-worth individual concerned about tax liability as well as asset growth and the protection of financial assets. Lawyers, trust officers, accountants, and/or advisors.

Cross Sell: Portfolio Management

→ Estate Planning
To assist in overall family financial planning

→ Brokerage Services
To buy and sell specific investments with (or without) advice

→ Mutual Funds
To offer a variety of risk levels and returns for the hands-on investor

→ Legal Services
To assist with trusts, wills, and certain tax matters

→ Sweep Investment Account
To maximize interest income

→ Business (or Personal) Money Market Account
As an alternative to standard checking—earns interest and is a convenient way to keep an accurate record of cash flow

→ Automatic Teller Machine (ATM)
To access funds at any hour, on any day, at locations worldwide

→ Home Equity Line of Credit
As a convenient way to have tax-advantaged funds available for a variety of purposes

---

→ Notes

Contacts	Department	Telephone

Pricing/Fees _____

Miscellaneous _____

Private Banking

An over-used description that has come to indicate almost any bank that has relationships with up-scale customers. Private banking means being assigned a person(s) who will monitor an investment portfolio, handle the taxes generated by the portfolio, and provide investment advice. These individuals (some work at private banks, others at trust companies) are referred to as trust officers; however, over the last decade, they have preferred to be called private bankers.

Ninety percent of the commercial banks in the United States offer some kind of private banking service. Often called trust services, portfolio management, or both, private banking is generally agreed to be a credit-investment-trust relationship formed with high-net-worth individuals.

The Customer

High-net-worth individuals—their lawyers, trust officers, accountants, advisors.

Cross Sell: Private Banking

→ **Brokerage Services**
To trade in the securities chosen

→ **Checking (Current) Account**
To provide depository for short-term funds

→ **Margin Account**
To maximize use of equity buying

→ **Estate Planning**
To assist in overall family financial planning

→ **Portfolio Management**
To assist in investment strategies and execution

→ **Mutual Funds**
To offer a variety of risk levels and returns for the hands-on investor

→ **Legal Services**
To assist with trusts, wills, and certain tax matters

→ **Foreign Sales Corporation (FSC) or International Business Corporation (IBC)**
To administer and manage tax-protected holdings

Notes

Contacts	Department	Telephone

Pricing/Fees _____

_____

_____

Miscellaneous _____

_____

Revolving Line of Credit

A commercial line of credit that allows a company to gain access to funds on an "as needed" basis for short-term borrowing purposes. It is usually granted only to those commercial customers whose character and capacity to repay have been firmly established. The amounts borrowed on a revolving line of credit generally must be repaid annually; thus, the borrower's needs for this line must be short-term. All lines require the personal guarantee of the principal(s) of the borrowing company.

Once the line is granted, financial statements of the company and of those personally guaranteeing the loan must be submitted to the bank on at least an annual basis.

The Customer

A financially sensitive business owner or a financial officer.

Cross Sell:
Revolving Line of Credit

➔ Business Checking
As a prerequisite, in most cases, to the line of credit

➔ Commercial Loan
To borrow for growth, debt consolidation, etc.

➔ Direct Deposit
To have employees' paychecks automatically deposited into their accounts

➔ Employee Checking
As a convenient way to provide banking services to employees

Notes

Contacts	Department	Telephone

Pricing/Fees _____

_____

_____

Miscellaneous _____

_____

_____

Safe Deposit Box

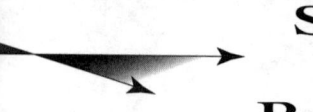

A secure place within a bank or financial institution to store valuables, such as papers, cash, and jewelry.

Customers are provided with a metal box, in a size of their choice, to which they hold the only key. Security for these boxes is strictly maintained by means of various precautions, which makes the service highly appealing to customers who need to protect or safeguard their valuables.

The financial institution charges for safe deposit boxes on an annual basis.

The Customer

Anyone concerned with safekeeping. Customers who purchase Certificates of Deposit (CDs), who write wills, or who buy insurance policies often seek this kind of secure place for their documents and bank notes.

Cross Sell:
Safe Deposit Box

➛Checking Account
For automatic debit of the annual fee

➛Automatic Teller Machine (ATM)
To access funds at any hour, on any day, at locations throughout the world

➛Direct Deposit
As the most reliable way to have paychecks deposited without going to the bank

➛ Notes

Contacts	Department	Telephone

Pricing/Fees ______________________________

____

____

Miscellaneous ______________________________

____

____

Savings Accounts

A statement savings account that reports its activity through monthly or quarterly statements by detailing all transactions made and interest earned. These accounts most often require a minimum average daily balance to avoid a maintenance fee. Interest is paid on all balances and compounded monthly or quarterly.

This account can be connected to direct deposit, which allows the customer to make deposits without visiting the bank.

The Customer

Usually an individual with a checking account who uses savings for special purposes, such as travel.

Cross Sell:
Savings Account

➔ Automatic Teller Machine (ATM)
To access funds at any hour, on any day, at locations worldwide

➔ Direct Deposit
As a safe way to have funds deposited

➔ Checking (Current) Account
To link with savings via the ATM card

➔ Home Equity Credit Line
As a fast, easy way to have tax-advantaged money available for major purchases

---

➤ Notes

Contacts	Department	Telephone

Pricing/Fees _____

Miscellaneous _____

Savings Bank Life Insurance (SBLI)

A variety of life insurance products endorsed by a savings bank in three states in the United States (Connecticut, Massachusetts, and New York).

These life insurance products are generally offered at a low cost to the customer because there are no agent commission and the product is sold by bankers who are not on sales commissions.

In terms of security, SBLI is rated "A+ Superior" by the A.M. Best Company, "Excellent" by Standard and Poor's.

Even though the products change from year to year, the following provides a current selection:

- **Yearly renewable term policy.** A term policy that is automatically renewable each year up to age 70 and is convertible to any SBLI permanent policy up to age 65.

- **Whole life policy.** A policy that starts building cash and loan value at the end of the first year and that sometimes provides liberal dividends.

- **Premium offset policy.** Premiums are paid out-of-pocket for a projected number of years, while dividends are left to purchase paid-up life additions or to accumulate interest. Future premiums are then paid by the dividend pool. Available on straight life, life paid up in twenty years, and life paid up at age sixty-five.

- **Lifesaver plan.** A single, premium-deferred annuity, designed for persons seeking an attractive total return on a tax-deferred basis. Provides safety of principal and the option of withdrawing accumulated funds.

- **Decreasing term policy.** A mortgage-cancellation protection policy or a special-purpose supplement for an insurance program.

- **Children's insurance policy.** Most SBLI policies are also available for children; however, premiums for children are much lower than those for adults and amounts are limited.

The Customer

Individuals seeking low-cost life insurance.

Cross Sell:
Savings Bank Life Insurance (SBLI)

→ **Certificates of Deposit (CDs)**
As a low-risk investment

→ **Individual Retirement Account**
As retirement funds to supplement income from social security

→ **IRA Savings**
As an easy, worry-free way to make sure IRA funds are available

→ **Annuities**
As tax-advantaged methods for withdrawing funds for retirement

→ **Estate Planning**
To assist in overall family financial planning

Notes

Contacts	Department	Telephone

Pricing/Fees _____

Miscellaneous _____

SBA (Small Business Administration) Loan

A commercial loan that banks make to small businesses and which the federal government guarantees. The guarantee allows the bank to grant loans that otherwise may not be approved. SBA loans usually have terms more favorable than those of nonguaranteed loans that are offered to small businesses. Once a loan application is approved by a bank's SBA loan department, it is sent to the SBA at the federal level for its review and approval.

SBA loans can be made for many purposes:

1. Purchasing existing businesses, start-up businesses, or equipment.

2. Purchasing commercial real estate.

3. Refinancing existing debt.

4. Securing working capital (as a short-term loan or line of credit).

SBA loans feature a variable rate that is indexed to the prime rate, as quoted in *The Wall Street Journal.*

The Customer

Small business owners who have responsibly researched their borrowing options and determined that an SBA loan is their best opportunity. In many cases, this preliminary research will provide documentation of their ability to repay.

Cross Sell:
SBA (Small Business Administration) Loan

⇾ Business Checking
As a convenient way to maintain a good banking relationship

⇾ Small Business Line of Credit
To save borrowing time and ensure funds availability

⇾ Employee Checking
As a convenient way to offer banking services to employees

⇾ Direct Deposit
To have the paychecks of employees automatically deposited into their accounts

---

Notes

Contacts	Department	Telephone

Pricing/Fees _____

_____

_____

Miscellaneous_____

_____

_____

Second Mortgage

A mortgage loan granted subsequent to an existing first residential mortgage.

The sum of the first and second mortgages cannot exceed 70 percent of the appraised value of the property. The interest rate on a second mortgage is fixed, for a term of five to fifteen years.

The Customer

Most will be from the area where they are buying the home, and will reflect the temperament for settling down for an extended period. Expect working parents with children.

Cross Sell: Second Mortgage

→ Credit Life Insurance
To pay off the mortgage in the event of the mortgagee's death

→ Equity Line of Credit
As a convenient, tax-advantaged way to make significant purchases

→ Checking (Current) Account
As a convenient way to make mortgage payments directly to the mortgagor

→ Automatic Payment
As an easier and more convenient way to make mortgage payments without having to write checks

→ Homeowner's Insurance
(Only available through banks in some countries) To protect the home against natural and other carefully stipulated disasters

---

→ Notes

Contacts	Department	Telephone

Pricing/Fees _____

Miscellaneous _____

Ship Registration

A service whereby a ship or yacht is legally registered for the owner in a jurisdiction where the assets and expenses of the ship will be least vulnerable to tax regulations.

The Customer

High-net-worth individuals or business managers associated with lucrative properties.

Cross Sell:
Ship Registration

→ Legal Services
To advise on tax and jurisdictional matters

→ International Business Corporations
To control tax vulnerability and serve as legal address for the ship

→ Checking or Money Market Depository
As a source for available funds

→ Online Balance Reporting
To improve funds management by monitoring account balances and transaction histories

→ Account Analysis
To consolidate activity from multiple accounts

➤ Notes

Contacts	Department	Telephone

Pricing/Fees _____

Miscellaneous _____

Simplified Employee Pension (SEP)

An employer-sponsored retirement plan in which IRAs are established for the benefit of each eligible employee and enriched by SEP contributions. This retirement vehicle requires little record keeping and minimal reporting to the government.

Employee participation can be limited to those who are twenty-one and over, and who have worked from three to five years for the sponsoring employer. The employer's contribution of up to $30,000, or 15 percent of each employee's compensation (whichever is less), is fully tax deductible, and contributions may vary from year to year.

A SEP is similar to an IRA, in that no withdrawals can be made until age 59 1/2 without a tax penalty; however, distributions must be made by age 70 1/2.

Employees participating in a SEP can take 100 percent of their SEP funds with them when they retire from the company.

The Customer

Businesses interested in providing retirement assistance to their employees.

Cross Sell:
Simplified Employee Pension (SEP)

⇾ Business Checking
To keep an accurate record of cash flow

⇾ Payroll Services
To reduce the time and cost of processing payroll for employees

⇾ Cash Management Services
To assist in maximizing interest income and minimizing banking fees

⇾ Trust Services
To provide expertise in the areas of investments and planning

---

Notes

Contacts	Department	Telephone

Pricing/Fees _____

_____

_____

Miscellaneous _____

_____

_____

Small Business Line of Credit

An unsecured line of credit for small businesses that is intended to cover short-term borrowing needs. When this product is attached to a business checking account, it can be used as overdraft protection.

The maximum amount of these small business credit lines varies, but is in the $25,000 range (depending on the bank). The interest on the line begins to accrue immediately after its first use. The interest rate on a line of credit is calculated through the bank's base rate plus a small percentage. Monthly payments on these lines can be debited from the customer's checking account.

This type of financial service allows the small business to have a reasonable-cost way to borrow funds or to cover overdrafts. Small businesses may borrow needed funds without having to endure the extended time and greater paperwork required for a commercial loan.

Most banks charge an annual fee, which varies widely by the institution.

The Customer

A small business owner who is knowledgeable about borrowing money and paying it back.

Cross Sell:
Small Business Line of Credit

➻ Business Checking
As a prerequisite to a small business loan

➻ Commercial Loan
To borrow for growth, debt consolidation, etc.

➻ Direct Deposit
To have employees' paychecks automatically deposited into their accounts

➻ Employee Checking
As a convenient way to provide banking services to employees

➤ Notes

Contacts	Department	Telephone

Pricing/Fees _____

_____

_____

Miscellaneous _____

_____

_____

Standby Letter of Credit

A bank's promise to back up a borrower's monetary guarantee to perform a certain service for (or pay a specified amount to) a designated beneficiary. A standby letter is a contingent liability of the bank: it ensures the borrower's performance of (or payment on) a contract, and thus forms part of the overall debt of the borrower. Although the bank fully expects the borrower to complete the performance of his or her obligation to the beneficiary, in the case of a default, it is the bank who must pay the beneficiary and seek reimbursement from the borrower.

There is a one-year maximum length of time for which a standby letter of credit should be written, and it must generally be secured by either marketable securities or other collateral that the bank deems acceptable. A complete credit review is required by the bank loan officer and/or credit analyst.

The fee for this service is a percentage of the amount of the letter of credit.

The Customer

Either an owner or financial officer of a company. Construction companies, developers, etc., may also approach banks for this kind of credit.

Cross Sell:
Standby Letter of Credit

➛ Business Checking
As a prerequisite for most commercial products

➛ Line of Credit
To save borrowing time and ensure funds availability

➛ Direct Deposit
To have employees' paychecks automatically deposited into their accounts

➛ Employee Checking
As a convenient way to offer banking services to employees

➤ Notes

Contacts	Department	Telephone

Pricing/Fees _____

_____

_____

Miscellaneous _____

_____

_____

Student Loans

There are three federal education loans available for students and/or parents who need to borrow for college tuition. (Also called education loans.) Guaranteed by the United States government, these loans are the following:

- Federal Stafford Loan (subsidized and unsubsidized)
- Federal Supplemental Loans for Students (SLS)
- Federal Parent PLUS Loan

Applications for these loans are generally available at most banks (the applications are supplied by Nellie Mae). The maximum loan amounts differ, based on the student's academic status. A student's eligibility for the loan is determined by the school's financial aid office, which requires the student to attend school at least half-time. Once approved, the funds are disbursed, in allotments, directly to the student's school, as dictated by the school or by Nellie Mae.

A guarantee fee and/or origination fee is deducted from the total amount when the loan is approved.

To ensure loan affordability, student loan rates are guaranteed by the federal government. The student (or parent) doesn't have to start repaying the loan until six months after the student either graduates or leaves school.

The Customer

Students and/or their parents seeking information and sources of financial aid.

Cross Sell: Student Loans

→Checking (Current) Account
To provide parents with an accurate record of cash flow; to provide students with a disciplined way to learn money management

→Automatic Teller Machine (ATM)
To access cash on any day, at any hour, at locations worldwide

→Statement Savings
To link the checking to the savings via the ATM card

→Equity Credit Line
As a supplemental source for funding education in a tax-advantaged way

---

Notes

Contacts	Department	Telephone

Pricing/Fees _____

Miscellaneous _____

Sweep Investment Account

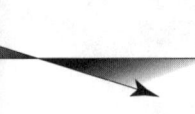

This service enables business customers to have their excess funds automatically invested on a daily basis. In general terms, funds that exceed $50,000 in a business checking account are swept automatically, the next day, into an external funding account.

Funds are swept automatically back into a business checking account when balances fall below the minimum level. Account statements reflect sweeps made to and from the money market mutual funds (available as account options on most sweep accounts).

This account is ideal for businesses with frequent funds-transfer activity. Accounts must have minimum balances of at least $50,000 to take advantage of this product.

Charges for this financial service include a monthly service fee as well as a monthly account analysis fee.

The Customer

Financially sensitive business owner or financial officer.

Cross Sell:
Sweep Investment Account

→ Online Balance Reporting
To improve funds management through monitoring account balances

→ Business Checking
As a convenient way to keep an accurate record of cash flow

→ Account Analysis
As an easy way to consolidate activity from multiple accounts

→ Business Credit Line
(Or revolving line of credit) to draw from on an as-needed basis

---

➤ Notes

Contacts	Department	Telephone
_____	_____	_____
_____	_____	_____
_____	_____	_____

Pricing/Fees _____

_____

_____

Miscellaneous_____

_____

_____

Tax-Free Money Market Fund

A mutual fund that invests in short-term municipal notes and bonds.

This type of fund is a low-risk investment, seeking tax-free income. Very often these funds are available with full checking services.

The Customer

Investment-conscious individuals who don't want to spend the time (or take the chance) buying and selling stocks, bonds, etc., and who need a depository for investment funds.

Cross Sell:
Tax-Free Money Market Fund

➔ Deposit Account
(Checking, money market or fund with checkbook) to accept dividends and income and to buy other investments

➔ Growth and/or Income Mutual Funds
To receive the investment money from the depository

➔ Margin Account
To buy when the research is convincing, regardless of the deposit account balance

➔ Credit Card
For travel, entertainment, and special purchases

➔ Retirement Accounts
To accept maximum contributions as defined by law

➔ Trust Services
For expertise in estate planning and investments

➤ Notes

Contacts	Department	Telephone

Pricing/Fees _____

Miscellaneous _____

Tax Services

This covers a broad category of services, such as:

- Fiduciary income tax returns
- Tax letters for custodial and individually managed portfolio accounts
- Estate tax returns
- Gift tax returns
- Charitable tax returns
- Nonresident alien tax returns
- Domestic employment tax returns
- Tax planning/analysis
- IRS and state audit engagements
- Preparation of ordinary income tax returns (1040s)

The Customer

Businesses large and small, and any individual needing assistance with tax matters.

Cross Sell:
Tax Services

⇾ Estate Planning
To assist in overall family financial planning

⇾ Trust Services
To provide expertise in the area of investments and planning

⇾ Legal Services
To assist with trusts, wills, and certain tax matters

⇾ Checking (Current) Account
To provide an accurate record of cash flow

⇾ Automatic Teller Machine (ATM)
To access funds at any hour, on any day, at thousands of locations worldwide

---

➤ Notes

Contacts	Department	Telephone

Pricing/Fees _____

_____

_____

Miscellaneous _____

_____

_____

TTL (Treasury, Tax and Loan Deposit)

A bank service that makes federal tax deposits for business customers.

Banks can process monthly tax payments made by corporations through their bank business accounts. To have the bank perform this service, the business customer writes a check to the bank, furnishing a form that indicates the type of tax to be paid. The bank then wires the payment for the identified tax on behalf of the customer. Most banks do not charge a fee for this service.

This convenient service can help businesses avoid costly IRS late penalties, and, in addition, guarantee them a complete record for any future research.

The Customer

Usually a bookkeeper or very small business owner.

Cross Sell:
TTL (Treasury, Tax and Loan Deposit)

→ Business Checking Account
As a prerequisite for this service

→ Payroll Processing
As a simplified way to manage the company payroll

→ Sweep Investment Account
To maximize interest income

→ Business Money Market Account
As an interest-earning alternative to standard business checking

---

► Notes

Contacts	Department	Telephone

Pricing/Fees _____

_____

_____

Miscellaneous _____

_____

_____

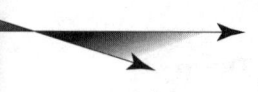

Traveler's Checks

A form of check designed for individuals who travel and don't want to risk carrying a lot of cash. These checks, which are redeemable at any bank or most places of business, are printed in varying denominations, from $10 to $100, and can be used to purchase goods and services almost anywhere cash is accepted.

The Customer

Tourists, travelers, businesspersons.

Cross Sell:
Traveler's Checks

↦ Checking (Current) Account
As a convenient way to pay bills and to keep an accurate record of cash flow

↦ Automatic Teller Machine (ATM)
To access funds at any hour, on any day, at locations worldwide

↦ Direct Deposit
As a safe way to have funds deposited in a deposit account

↦ Savings Account
To link to the checking account via the ATM card

→ Notes

Contacts	Department	Telephone

Pricing/Fees _____

_____

_____

Miscellaneous _____

_____

_____

Treasurer's Checks

A check signed by a bank cashier that makes it a direct obligation of the bank. (Also called a cashier's check.) Treasurer's checks are for amounts over $1,000.

The Customer

An individual who needs to pay in guaranteed funds other than cash.

Cross Sell:
Treasurer's Checks

↠ Checking (Current) Account
As a convenient way to pay bills and keep an accurate record of cash flow

↠ Automatic Teller Machine (ATM)
To access funds at any hour, on any day, at locations worldwide

↠ Direct Deposit
As a safe way to have funds deposited in an account

↠ Savings Account
To link to the checking account via the ATM card

Notes

Contacts	Department	Telephone

Pricing/Fees _____

Miscellaneous _____

Trust Services

A broad range of trust (or fiduciary) services primarily dealing with the handling of wealth, providing expertise on how to invest and how to protect investments. Specifically such products/services as acting as trustee, living wills, revocable/nonrevocable trusts, etc., are the bailiwick of the bank's trust services department.

Not only is the appropriate mix of products/services an integral part of this service, but the personality and perceived level of competence of the trust officer is the most important part of this service.

The Customer

Anyone who has accumulated some assets and either isn't interested in managing those assets or doesn't feel comfortable with the task of asset management.

Cross Sell:
Trust Services

→ Money Market Account
To function as a depository for investments

→ Automatic Teller Machine (ATM)
To access funds at any hour, on any day, at locations worldwide

→ Equity Credit Line
As a convenient way to have tax-advantaged funds available for investments

→ Checking (Current) Account
As a convenient way to keep an accurate record of cash flow and to link to a money market account via the ATM card

→ Estate Planning
To assist in overall family financial planning

→ Notes

Contacts	Department	Telephone

Pricing/Fees _____

_____

_____

Miscellaneous _____

_____

_____

U.S. Government Money Market Fund

A mutual fund that invests entirely in treasury and agency issues.

In most cases this type of fund offers a checkbook and is the recipient of dividend payments and sales of stocks or other mutual funds.

A money market fund is a very low risk investment, with a return only slightly higher than a bank Certificate of Deposit (CD).

The Customer

The investment-conscious use this fund as a "catchall" for investment income and/or sales. Also retirement-age individuals use this fund as another conservative investment.

Cross Sell:
U.S. Government Money Market Fund

→ Checking (Current) Account
To provide depository for short-term funds

→ Growth and/or Income Mutual Funds
To receive the investment money from the depository

→ Margin Account
To buy when the research is convincing, regardless of the deposit account balance

→ Credit Card
For travel, entertainment, and special purchases

→ Retirement Account
To accept maximum contributions as defined by law

→ Trust Services
For expertise in estate planning and investments

➤ Notes

Contacts	Department	Telephone

Pricing/Fees _____

Miscellaneous _____

U.S. Savings Bonds

These bonds can be purchased only through the United States government and cannot be traded among investors. Many conservative investors refer to them as "EE bonds."

One buys these bonds at a discount from par value and, upon maturity, the government pays the full face amount. In actuality, these savings bonds are the original zero-coupon bonds.

These instruments are sold from the United States Treasury and purchased primarily through banks.

Par value for EE bonds is $50 to $10,000, with an adjustable maturity. Par value for HH bonds is $500 to $10,000, with a 10-year maturity.

The Customer

Very conservative investors buy these bonds. Also, people who give gifts of money to their children and grandchildren favor this kind of purchase.

Cross Sell:
U.S. Savings Bonds

↳ Certificate Of Deposit (CD)
As a low-risk investment for a portion of one's funds

↳ Direct Deposit
As a safe way to have funds deposited without going to the bank

↳ Checking (Current) Account
As an account for receiving deposits and for writing checks

→ Notes

Contacts	Department	Telephone

Pricing/Fees _____

_____

_____

Miscellaneous _____

_____

_____

Vehicle Dealership Financing

Banks will help dealerships finance their inventory of new and used cars and trucks, new and used boats, motorcycles, motor homes, and recreational vehicles. Often called "floor plan lines," this financing depends on the sale of vehicle inventory for repayment of the loan; proceeds of a vehicle sale are applied to the dealer's loan balance.

A vehicle that a dealer puts into inventory with floor plan financing must have the bill of sale and/or title. Such borrowing causes dealers to build high levels of debt and to rely heavily on collateral; thus, the bank exercises careful procedural control, including monthly audits, over the collateral.

Vehicle dealership borrowers are encouraged to maintain a deposit relationship with the bank in order to facilitate advances and repayments; of course, the bank uses this relationship to closely control the loan. Lines of credit to dealers are reviewed and renewed annually, once the bank has analyzed current financial statements.

The Customer

Automobile dealers and some boat dealers.

Cross Sell:
Vehicle Dealership Financing

➜ Business Checking Account
As a prerequisite for this type of financing

➜ Line of Credit
To save borrowing time and ensure funds availability

➜ Direct Deposit
To have company paychecks for employees automatically deposited into their accounts

➜ Employee Checking Account
As a convenient, easy way to provide banking services to a company's employees

---

➤ Notes

Contacts	Department	Telephone

Pricing/Fees _____

_____

_____

Miscellaneous _____

_____

_____

 # Wills

A legal document carefully written to conform to local, state, and federal laws regarding the passing of one's estate at death. Over the years (and from country to country) individuals have written and rewritten laws pertaining to inheritances, and the execution of a will always has to take into consideration any new laws.

Even though there exist computer software programs that print "off-the-shelf" wills, in most cases, drawing up a will is the province of attorneys who are knowledgeable about their state's legal inheritance issues.

Wills can be created at law offices and in many trust departments of banks, as well as at trust companies and other specialized institutions.

The Customer

Individuals who have determined which possessions they would like to leave in the event of their death and are therefore seeking professional expertise.

Cross Sell:
Wills

→ Estate Planning
To organize and assist in overall family financial planning

→ Brokerage Services
To purchase equities or bonds for the estate

→ Portfolio Management
As an alternative to brokerage services, if The Customer's estate is sizable

→ Money Market Account
To serve as a depository for investments or investment returns

→ Automatic Teller Machine (ATM)
To access funds at any hour, on any day, at locations worldwide

---

➤ Notes

Contacts	Department	Telephone

Pricing/Fees _____

_____

_____

Miscellaneous _____

_____

_____

Wire Transfers

The process of electronically transferring monies from one bank to another, anywhere in the world.

A wire transfer can move money from one account in one bank to another account in another bank more quickly than any other means. It not only avoids the slowness and frequent unreliability of the mail but also eliminates float delays on time-sensitive matters.

Wire-transfer timing is critical, since all banks have cutoff times in their wire-transfer room.

Pricing on this service is done per transaction—incoming as well as outgoing. Wire transfers are an expensive service, but they satisfy time-sensitive financial needs.

The Customer

Business owners and financial officers favor wire transfers. Businesses use wire transfers to get quick payment of an invoice. Individuals also use them, particularly to wire money for emergencies.

Cross Sell:
Wire Transfers

↠ Business Checking
As a convenient way to keep an accurate record of cash flow

↠ Line of Credit
To save borrowing time and ensure funds availability

↠ Payroll Direct Deposit
As an easy, hassle-free way to deposit employees' paychecks

↠ Travel Credit Card
To control travel and entertainment expenses

→ Notes

Contacts	Department	Telephone

Pricing/Fees _____

_____

_____

Miscellaneous_____

_____

_____

Zero Balance Account

An account typically set up to keep bank balances at "0," except when items are presented for payment, in which case funds are transferred automatically from another account to cover the items presented. After nightly posting, any excess balances in this account are drawn down to "0" and transferred back to the funding account.

This is an account that charges a fee, and it is used by companies whose cash flow might be erratic, resulting in high balances one month and low balances the next. In order to maximize their monies, companies can keep excess funds in accounts that pay liberal interest—until they are needed.

The Customer

Larger businesses dealing in irregular influxes of cash, oftentimes against a line of credit.

Cross Sell:
Zero Balance Account

↣ Sweep Investment Account
To automatically move excess funds to accounts earning higher interest

↣ Commercial Loans
To provide funds for growth, etc.

↣ Employee Benefits
To provide a full range of retirement and profit sharing programs

↣ Payroll Services
To reduce the time and cost of processing payroll for employees

---

Notes

Contacts	Department	Telephone

Pricing/Fees _____

_____

_____

Miscellaneous _____

_____

_____

Appendix

Confidentiality

The issue of client confidentiality is one that (of late) has been "watered down," or compromised seriously. Many people look at the concept of confidentiality as negative, in terms of a banker or fiduciary officer trying to hide something illegal. Having worked in the financial/fiduciary services business for twenty-five years, this author has seen the dangers of compromise with this serious issue.

Perhaps one of the most outspoken and articulate people on the issue of confidentiality is Mr. Christopher G. Smeets, chairman and chief executive officer of The Citco Group Limited, a substantial conglomerate of banks and trust companies located throughout the world. In that company's most recent corporate capabilities brochure, Mr. Smeets outlined his feelings about the issue of confidentiality and I reprint the entire document with permission, as a simple way to understand a statement on this issue:

The Individual's Right to Privacy

The first philosophers of western civilization defined the individual's right to civil liberties, which were later embodied in all democratic constitutions. One of these rights, thus guaranteed, is the basic concept of the individual's right to privacy.

Privacy is a multidimensional issue. One dimension is where one party, by the nature of the relationship, has to respect the privacy of the other party and therefore protect that privacy by keeping information confidential. This right of privacy has also been a cornerstone of the legal and medical professions, as well as in an individual's relationship with the clergy.

The Derivation of Financial Confidentiality

The principle of financial confidentiality was incorporated in ancient law and again codified in Europe in the Middle Ages. Through the centuries—especially in times of political turmoil, civil unrest, and wars—confidence in the discretion of bankers became indispensable for the protection of private property and the proper conduct of commerce. By the middle of the 19th century, the confidentiality of banking records and bank information had been accepted by almost all of the nations of Europe.

In this century during periods of world upheaval and violent regional conflicts, many persons, under threat of persecution, were protected by the legitimate right to confidentiality of financial records in various countries; thus, many estates were preserved. Nevertheless, to this day, such threats to personal liberty and private ownership as confiscation of assets, confiscatory taxation, forced repatriation, and extreme forced heirship laws continue to occur.

Confidentiality of financial information was never absolute and is not a right of criminals. The changing attitudes in the last decades to this issue of confidentiality, especially among judicial authorities, have caused conflicts and, in certain instances, eroded this right of privacy. The fact that criminals will abuse any financial system should not result in the sacrifice of the principle of a banker's fiduciary obligation to his client's right to confidentiality of information.

Serving the Customer and Abiding by the Law

Banks conduct their business and their clients' business within the framework of the law, albeit the banker may not always agree with the rules and regulations created by the lawgivers or the executives of government. In abiding by those rules, bankers should live up to the tradition of their professional and fiduciary responsibilities to protect their clients' legitimate rights to confidentiality. The statutory and legitimate right of the magistrate to secure evidence in the prosecution of criminals will prevail when in conflict with the banker's fiduciary obligation; but it must be balanced with respect for the rights of innocent bystanders to safeguard their assets. Thus, in a world of changing opinions and attitudes with respect to confidential information and the erosion of individual liberties in pursuit of criminals, a banker's responsibility towards the protection of his clients' information appears to have had its foundation in law diminished.

1996–1997 Global Economic Outlook Chart

How to use this chart: Reference the business section of your newspaper for each of the indicators listed. Write the monthly figures in the box below the month. Keep track of the trend in each of the indicators for the markets in which you serve.

Country: United States	1996			1997										
Performance Measure	OCT	NOV	DEC	JAN	FEB	MAR	APR	MAY	JUN	JUL	AUG	SEP	OCT	NOV	DEC
Gross Domestic Product percentage change															
Unemployment Rate as a percent															
Sensitive Materials Pricing percentage change															
Interest Rates as a percent															
Stock Market percentage change															

Country:

Performance Measure	1996			1997											
	OCT	NOV	DEC	JAN	FEB	MAR	APR	MAY	JUN	JUL	AUG	SEP	OCT	NOV	DEC
Gross Domestic Product percentage change															
Unemployment Rate as a percent															
Sensitive Materials Pricing percentage change															
Interest Rates as a percent															
Stock Market percentage change															

Country:

Performance Measure	1996			1997											
	OCT	NOV	DEC	JAN	FEB	MAR	APR	MAY	JUN	JUL	AUG	SEP	OCT	NOV	DEC
Gross Domestic Product percentage change															
Unemployment Rate as a percent															
Sensitive Materials Pricing percentage change															
Interest Rates as a percent															
Stock Market percentage change															

Market Trends: Illustrative Annual Rates of Return

Common Stocks (S&P 500)—Standard and Poor's Composite Index, an unmanaged weighted index of the stock performance of 500 industrial, transportation, utility and financial companies.

Long-term Government Bonds—Measured using a one-bond portfolio constructed each year containing a bond with approximately a twenty year maturity and a reasonably current coupon.

Long-term Corporate Bonds—For the period 1969-1990, represented by the Salomon Brothers Long-term, High-Grade Corporate Bond Index; for the period 1946-1968, the Salomon Brothers Index was backdated using Salomon Brothers monthly yield data and a methodology similar to that used by Salomon Brothers for 1969-1990; for the period 1925-1945, the Standard and Poor's monthly High-Grade Corporate Composite yield data were used, assuming a 4 percent coupon and a twenty year maturity.

Intermediate-term Government Bonds—Measured by a one-bond portfolio constructed each year containing a bond with approximately a five year maturity.

U.S. Treasury Bills—Measured by rolling over each month a one-bill portfolio containing, at the beginning of each month, the bill having the shortest maturity not less than one month.

Inflation—Measured by the Consumer Price Index for all Urban Consumers (CPI-U), not seasonally adjusted.

For the following periods ending 12/31/95: Stocks	Small Company Stocks	Large Company Bonds	Long-Term Corporate Bonds	Intermediate-Term Govt. Bonds	U.S. Treasury Bills	Inflation
1 Year	34.3%	37.4%	27.2%	16.8%	5.6%	2.7%
3 Years	18.8	15.3	10.7	7.2	4.1	2.7
5 Years	24.5	16.6	12.2	8.8	4.3	2.8
10 Years	11.9	14.8	11.3	9.1	5.6	3.5
20 Years	19.6	14.6	10.6	9.5	7.3	5.2
30 Years	14.1	10.7	8.2	8.4	6.7	5.4
40 Years	14.4	10.8	6.4	7.0	5.7	4.5
50 Years	13.8	11.9	5.1	5.9	4.8	4.4
Since 01/01/26	10.9	10.5	5.7	5.3	3.7	3.1

Source: © Compiled using data from *Stocks, Bonds, Bills, and Inflation 1996 Yearbook*™, Ibbotson Associates, Chicago (Annually updates work by Roger G. Ibbotson and Rex A. Sinquefield). Used with permission. All rights reserved.

Index

A

Account analysis	2-3
asset-based lending and,	17
electronic banking interface and,	53
electronic depository transfer and,	55
employee benefits services and,	57
factoring and,	63
forward contracts and,	71
international fund administration and,	97
international letter of credit and,	99
ship registration and,	175
sweep investment account and,	185
Accounting services	
administration of companies and,	77
Internal Revenue Service reporting service and,	105
international business companies and,	95
merchant banking and,	119
Account reconciliation,	4–5
Adjustable-rate mortgages,	8–9
Administration of companies, general,	76–77
Aggressive growth fund,	10–11
A. M. Best Company,	168
Annuities,	12–13
life insurance and,	113, 115, 169
pension fund and,	151
Anticipation notes,	128
Asset allocation fund,	14–15
See also Balanced fund	
Asset-based lending,	16-17, 139
Automated clearinghouse,	52, 54
Automatic payment	
adjustable-rate mortgages and,	9
automobile loans and,	19
bank-by-mail and,	25
construction loans and,	47, 153
first-time home buyer and,	65
fixed-rate mortgages and,	69
home equity line of credit and,	85
home equity loan and,	87
land loan and,	109
second mortgage and,	173
Automatic teller machine	
automobile loans and,	19
bank-by-mail and,	25

Automatic teller machine (continued)
- brokerage services and, ... .31
- certificates of deposit and, ... .37
- checking accounts and, ... 33, 39
- Christmas Club and, ... .41
- construction loan and, ... .47
- direct deposit and, ... .51
- estate planning services and, ... .61
- estate settlement services and, ... .59
- first-time home buyer and, ... .65
- home improvement loans and, ... .89
- individually managed portfolios and, ... .91
- individual retirement account (IRA) and, ... .93
- investment management and, ... 101
- life insurance and, ... 113, 115
- Mastercard/Visa and, ... 117
- money market accounts and, ... 35, 121
- money order and, ... 125
- notary public and, ... 135
- NOW account and, ... 137
- overdraft protection and, ... 143
- passbook loans and, ... 145
- pension fund and, ... 151
- personal line of credit and, ... 155
- portfolio management and, ... 159
- safe deposit box and, ... 165
- savings account and, ... 167
- student loans and, ... 183
- tax services and, ... 189
- traveler's checks and, ... 193
- treasurer's checks, ... 195
- trust services and, ... 157, 197
- wills and, ... 205

Automatic teller machine card, ... 20–21
Automatic transfer of funds, ... .41
Automobile loans, ... 18–19

B

Balanced fund, ... 22–23
Bank-by-mail, ... 24–25
Bank depository services, ... 77, 95
Banking, private, ... 160–161
Biweekly mortgage, ... .64
Bond fund, municipal, ... 126–127
Bond mutual funds, ... 27, 28–29, 66–67

Bonds, ...30
    corporate and municipal, ...26–27
    rates of return for, ...218, 219
    U.S. savings, ...148, 200–201
Bonds processing, payroll, ...148–149
Brokerage services, ...30–31
    acting as trustee and, ...7
    asset allocation fund and, ...15
    balanced fund and, ...23
    bond mutual funds and, ...29
    custodial accounts and, ...49
    estate services and, ...59, 61
    investment management and, ...101
    life insurance and, ...113, 115
    merchant banking and, ...119
    pension fund and, ...151
    personal trust service and, ...157
    portfolio management and, ...159
    private banking and, ...161
    municipal bond fund and, ...127
    wills and, ...205
Brokers, ...30

C

Cash management services, ...177
Certificates of deposit, ...36–37, 78, 92
    annuities and, ...13
    individual retirement account savings and, ...103
    Keogh plans and, ...107
    passbook savings and, ...147
    payroll bonds processing and, ...149
    savings bank life insurance and, ...169
    U.S. savings bonds and, ...201
Checking accounts (current accounts), ...38–39
    account reconciliation and, ...5
    acting as trustee and, ...7
    adjustable-rate mortgages and, ...9
    automatic teller machine cards and, ...21
    automobile loans and, ...19
    brokerage services and, ...31
    certificates of deposit and, ...37
    Christmas Club and, ...41
    construction loans and, ...47, 153
    custodial accounts and, ...49
    direct deposit and, ...51

Checking accounts (current accounts) (continued)
- estate planning services and, ...61
- estate settlement services and, ...59
- first-time home buyer and, ...65
- fixed-rate mortgages and, ...69
- foreign sales corporations and, ...75
- home equity line of credit and, ...85
- home equity loan and, ...87
- home improvement loans and, ...89
- individually managed portfolios and, ...91
- individual retirement account and, ...93, 103
- Keogh plans and, ...107
- land loan and, ...109
- Mastercard/Visa and, ...117
- merchant banking and, ...119
- money market account and, ...121
- money order and, ...125
- notary public and, ...135
- overdraft protection and, ...143
- passbook loans and, ...145
- personal line of credit and, ...155
- private banking and, ...161
- safe deposit box and, ...165
- savings account and, ...167
- second mortgage and, ...173
- student loans and, ...183
- tax services and, ...189
- traveler's checks and, ...193
- treasurer's checks, ...195
- trust services and, ...157, 197
- U.S. government money market fund and, ...199
- U.S. savings bonds and, ...201

Checking accounts, business, ...32–33
- asset-based lending and, ...17
- commercial loan and, ...43
- commercial mortgage and, ...45
- electronic banking interface and, ...53
- electronic depository transfer and, ...55
- employee-benefits services and, ...57
- factoring and, ...63
- forward contracts and, ...71
- revolving line of credit and, ...163
- simplified employee pension and, ...177
- small business administration loan and, ...171
- small-business line of credit and, ...179

Checking accounts, business, (continued)
    standby letter of credit and, ...181
    sweep investment account and, ...184, 185
    treasury, tax, and loan deposit (TTL) and, ...191
    vehicle dealership financing and, ...203
    wire transfers and, ...207

Checking accounts, employee
    asset-based lending and, ...17
    commercial loan and, ...43
    commercial mortgage and, ...45
    employee-benefits services and, ...57
    factoring and, ...63
    revolving line of credit and, ...163
    small business administration loan and, ...171
    small-business line of credit and, ...179
    standby letter of credit and, ...181
    vehicle dealership financing and, ...203

Checking or money market depository, ...97, 99, 175
Christmas Club, ...40–41
Cirrus, ...20
Citco Group Limitied, The, ...212
Commercial banking service, ...4

Commercial loans
    business checking account and, ...33
    business money market account and, ...35
    foreign sales corporations and, ...75
    forward contracts and, ...71
    late deposit window and, ...111
    merchant banking and, ...119
    night depository bags and, ...133
    revolving line of credit and, ...163
    small-business line of credit and, ...179
    zero balance account, ...209

Commercial mortgage, ...44–45
Commissions, ...30
Computerized funds transfer, ...73, 139
Confidentiality, ...212–214
Construction loans, ...46–47
    land loan and, ...109
    permanent, ...152–153

Credit cards
    account analysis and, ...3
    account reconciliation and, ...5
    administration of companies and, ...77
    aggressive growth fund and, ...11

Credit cards (continued)
    asset allocation fund and, ...15
    balanced fund and, ...23
    bond mutual funds and, ...29, 67
    business checking account and, ...33
    business money market account and, ...35
    corporate and municipal bonds and, .27
    equity-income fund and, ...67
    foreign exchange and, ...73
    growth and income fund and, ...83
    growth fund and, ...81
    international business companies and, ...95
    Mastercard/Visa, ...116–117
    merchant banking and, ...119
    money market fund and, ...79, 123
    municipal bond fund and, ...127
    mutual funds and, ...131
    on-line balance sheet reporting and, ...139
    option income fund and, ...141
    tax-free money market fund and, ...187
    travel, ...207
    U.S. government money market fund and, ...199

Credit life insurance
    fixed-rate mortgages and, ...69
    home equity line of credit and, ...85
    home equity loan and, ...87
    second mortgage and, ...173

Credit line; see Line of credit
Current account; see Checking accounts (current accounts)
Custodial accounts, ...48—49
Customers
    accountants, ...58, 60, 158, 160
    attorneys, ...6, 58, 60, 118, 158, 160
    automobile purchasers, ...18
    bankers (merchant), ...118
    bookkeepers, ...2, 4, 52, 104, 190
    business; see Customers, business
    conscientious, ...40, 102
    employees, ...38, 50, 106, 120, 136, 172
    financial institutions, ...118
    financial officers; see Customers, services for financial officers
    general; see Customers, services for general
    high-net-worth; see Customers, services for high-net-worth
    high-risk investors, ...10, 66
    home builder, ...46

Customers (continued)

home buyers,	64, 68, 172
homeowner's,	84, 86, 88
ill, disabled, and invalid,	24
investment-conscious; see Customers, services for investment-conscious	
low-risk to no-risk,	26, 36, 112, 114, 200
managers of funds and/or money markets,	96
middle-aged,	58, 60, 90, 92, 150, 156, 158, 182
municipalities or other governmental agencies,	128
older,	8, 12, 40, 50, 146, 150
speculative,	66, 80, 140
tax specialist,	104
time-conscious,	10, 24, 50, 66, 80, 82, 130, 140
tourists,	72, 192
traders,	72
traveler's,	192
trust officers,	6, 58, 60, 158, 160
trust services,	6, 156
two-income families with children,	68
without checking accounts,	124
younger,	8, 64, 92, 154, 182

Customers, business

automobile and boat dealers,	202
concerned with maximizing income,	34
construction developers/builders,	44, 108, 152, 180
exporters,	74
financially sensitive,	54, 162, 184
in general,	32, 42, 104, 110, 138, 148, 192, 206
international,	70
large and small,	176, 188
managers of lucrative properties,	174
medium-to-large,	16, 56, 62, 176, 208
off-shore,	76, 94
retail,	132, 176
small,	170, 176, 178, 180, 190
and their employees,	106

Customers, services for financial officers

account analysis,	2
account reconciliation,	4
business checking account,	32
business money market account,	34
electronic banking interface,	52
electronic depository transfer,	54
Internal Revenue Service reporting service,	104

Customers, services for financial officers (continued)
- international letter of credit, ... 98
- late deposit window, ... 110
- on-line balance reporting, ... 138
- payroll bonds processing, ... 148
- revolving line of credit, ... 162
- standby letter of credit, ... 180
- sweep investment account, ... 184
- wire transfers, ... 206

Customers, services for general
- asset management assistance, ... 100, 196
- automatic teller machine (ATM) card, ... 20
- credit cards, ... 116
- guaranteed funds, ... 194
- life insurance, ... 112, 169
- money market accounts, ... 120
- notary public, ... 134
- NOW account, ... 136
- overdraft protection, ... 142
- passbook loans, ... 144
- personal line of credit, ... 154
- safe deposit box, ... 164
- savings account, ... 166
- tax services, ... 188
- traveler's checks, ... 192
- wills, ... 204

Customers, services for high-net-worth
- administration of companies, ... 76
- brokerage services, ... 30
- estate planning services, ... 60
- estate settlement services, ... 58
- international business companies, ... 94
- merchant banking, ... 118
- personal trust services, ... 156
- portfolio management, ... 158
- private banking, ... 160
- ship registration, ... 174

Customers, services for investment-conscious
- asset allocation fund, ... 14
- balanced fund, ... 22
- bond mutual funds, ... 28
- brokerage services, ... 30
- custodial accounts, ... 48
- land loan, ... 108
- money market fund (general), ... 78, 122

229

Customers, services for investment-conscious (continued)
- municipal bond fund, ...126
- permanent construction loans, ...152
- tax-free money market fund, ...186
- U.S. government money market fund, ...198

D

Deposit account
- aggressive growth fund and, ...11
- asset allocation fund and, ...15
- balanced fund and, ...23
- bond mutual funds and, ...29, 67
- equity-income fund and, ...67
- growth and income fund and, ...83
- growth fund and, ...81
- money market, ...3
- municipal bond fund and, ...127

Deposit account
- mutual funds and, ...131
- option income fund and, ...141
- tax-free money market fund and, ...187

Depositories
- checking or money market, ...97, 99, 175
- merchant banking and, ...119

Direct deposit, ...50–51
- asset-based lending and, ...17
- automatic teller machine cards and, ...21
- bank-by-mail and, ...25
- checking (current) account and, ...39
- Christmas Club and, ...41
- commercial loan and, ...43
- commercial mortgage and, ...45
- employee-benefits services and, ...57
- factoring and, ...63
- first-time home buyer and, ...65
- home improvement loans and, ...89
- money market account and, ...121
- money order and, ...125
- night depository bags and, ...133
- notary public and, ...135
- NOW account and, ...137
- overdraft protection and, ...143
- passbook loans and, ...145
- passbook savings and, ...147
- personal line of credit and, ...155

Direct deposit, (continued)
- revolving line of credit and, ...163
- safe deposit box and, ...165
- savings account and, ...167
- small business administration loan and, ...171
- small-business line of credit and, ...179
- standby letter of credit and, ...181
- traveler's checks and, ...193
- treasurer's checks and, ...195
- U.S. savings bonds and, ...201
- vehicle dealership financing and, ...203

E

Earnings allowance credits, ...2
Economic outlook chart, global, ...214—217
Electronic banking interface, ...52-53, 105
Electronic depository transfer, ...54–55
Electronic funds transfer (EFT), ...50
Employee benefits services, ...56–57
- Internal Revenue Service reporting service and, ...105
- payroll bonds processing and, ...149
- zero balance account, ...209

Equities, 27, 30, 218, 219
Equity-income and fixed-income funds, ...66—67
Equity line of credit; see Line of credit, equity
Estate planning, ...60–61
- acting as trustee and, ...7
- brokerage services and, ...31
- custodial accounts and, ...49
- individually managed portfolios and, ...91
- individual retirement account and, ...93, 103
- investment management and, ...101
- Keogh plans and, ...107
- life insurance and, ...113, 115, 169
- pension fund and, ...151
- portfolio management and, ...159
- municipal bond fund and, ...127
- mutual funds and, ...131
- private banking and, ...161
- tax services and, ...189
- trust services and, ...157, 197
- wills and, ...205

Estate settlement services, ...58-59
Express 24, 20

F

Factoring, ... 62–63
First-mortgage refinancing, ... 85, 87
Fixed-income and equity income funds, ... 66–67
Fixed-rate mortgages, ... 68–69
Foreign currencies; see Forward contracts
Foreign exchange, ... 72–73
Foreign sales corporation (FSC), ... 74–75
    acting as trustee and, ... 7
    forward contracts and, ... 71
    private banking and, ... 161
Forward contracts, ... 70–71
    administration of companies and, ... 77
    foreign sales corporations and, ... 75
    international business companies and, ... 95
    international fund administration and, ... 97
    international letter of credit and, ... 99

G

Graduated payment mortgages, ... 68
Growth and/or income mutual funds, ... 82–83
    asset allocation fund and, ... 15
    balanced fund and, ... 23
    bond mutual funds and, ... 29
    money market fund and, ... 79, 123
    municipal bond fund and, ... 127
    tax-free money market fund and, ... 187
    U.S. government money market fund and, ... 199
Growth funds, ... 10–11, 80–81

H

Home buyer, first-time, ... 64–65
Home equity line of credit; see Line of credit,
Home equity loan, ... 86–87
Home improvement loans, ... 88
Homeowner's insurance
    fixed-rate mortgages and, ... 69
    home equity line of credit and, ... 85
    home equity loan and, ... 8
    home improvement loans and, ... 89
    life insurance and, ... 113, 115
    pension fund and, ... 151
    second mortgage and, ... 173

I

Ibbotson, Roger G., ... 219
Ibbotson Associates, ... 219n
Income fund, option, ... 140–141
Individually managed accounts, ... 90–91
Individual retirement accounts, ... 12, 92–93
    annuities and, ... 13
    savings bank life insurance and, ... 169
Individual retirement account savings, ... 102–103, 169
Inflation, annual rates of, ... 218, 219
Insurance
    adjustable-rate mortgages and, ... 9
    credit; see Credit life insurance
    homeowner's; see Homeowner's insurance
    life; see Life insurance
Internal Revenue Service reporting service, ... 104–105
International business corporation, ... 94–95
    acting as trustee and, ... 7
    forward contracts and, ... 71
    international fund administration and, ... 97
    private banking and, ... 161
    ship registration and, ... 175
International fund administration, ... 96–97
International letter of credit, ... 98–99
Investment management, ... 100–102
    see also Portfolio management

K

Keogh plans, ... 106–107

L

Land loan, ... 108–109
Late deposit window, ... 110–111
Legal services
    acting as trustee and, ... 7
    brokerage services and, ... 31
    custodial accounts and, ... 49
    estate planning services and, ... 61
    estate settlement services and, ... 59
    foreign sales corporations and, ... 75
    forward contracts and, ... 71
    international fund administration and, ... 97
    international letter of credit and, ... 99
    investment management and, ... 101

Legal services (continued)
- life insurance and, ... 113, 115
- merchant banking and, ... 119
- pension fund and, ... 151
- personal trust service and, ... 157
- portfolio management and, ... 159
- private banking and, ... 161
- ship registration and, ... 175
- tax services and, ... 189

Lending, asset-based, ... 16-17, 139

Life insurance, ... 112-113
- annuities and, ... 13
- credit; see Credit life insurance
- savings bank, ... 168-169

Life insurance trust, ... 114–115

Line of credit
- asset-based, ... 16, 17
- business; see Line of credit, business
- business checking account and, ... 33
- business money market account and, ... 35
- commercial loan and, ... 43
- commercial mortgage and, ... 45
- employee benefits services and, ... 57
- equity; see Line of credit, equity
- factoring and, ... 63
- forward contracts and, ... 71
- home equity; see Line of credit, home equity
- Internal Revenue Service reporting service and, ... 105
- late deposit window and, ... 111
- night depository bags and, ... 133
- personal, ... 154–155, 142
- revolving, ... 55, 162–163
- standby letter of credit and, ... 181
- vehicle dealership financing and, ... 203
- wire transfers and, ... 207

Line of credit, business
- account analysis and, ... 3
- account reconciliation and, ... 5
- electronic banking interface and, ... 53
- electronic depository transfer and, ... 55
- small-, ... 171, 178–179
- sweep investment account and, ... 185

Line of credit, equity
- adjustable-rate mortgages and, ... 9
- bank-by-mail and, ... 25

Line of credit, equity (continued)
- fixed-rate mortgages and, ... .69
- money market account and, ... .121
- NOW account and, ... .137
- second mortgage and, ... .173
- student loan and, ... .183
- trust services and, ... .197

Line of credit, home equity, ...84–85
- automobile loans and, ... .19
- individual retirement account savings and, ... .103
- investment management and, ... .101
- Keogh plans and, ... .107
- life insurance and, ... .113
- overdraft protection and, ... .143
- personal line of credit and, ... .155
- personal trust service and, ... .157
- portfolio management and, ... .159
- savings account and, ... .167

Loans; see also Credit cards; Line of credit; Margin account; Mortgages; Overdraft protection
- asset-based, ...16–17, 139
- automobile, ...18–19
- commercial; see Commercial loans
- construction; see Construction loans
- to finance vehicle dealerships, ...202–203
- home equity, ...86–87
- home improvement, ... .88
- land, ...108–109
- passbook, ...144–145
- personal, ... .103, 107
- student, ...182–183

M

Margin account
- acting as trustee and, ...7
- aggressive growth fund and, ... .11
- asset allocation fund and, ... .15
- balanced fund and, ... .23
- bond mutual funds and, ... .29, 67
- custodial accounts and, ... .49
- equity-income fund and, ... .67
- growth and income fund and, ... .83
- growth fund and, ... .81
- money market fund and, ... .79, 123
- municipal bond fund and, ... .127

Margin account (continued)
- mutual funds and, ... 131
- option income fund and, ... 141
- private banking and, ... 161
- tax-free money market fund and, ... 187
- U.S. government money market fund and, ... 199

Mastercard/Visa, ... 116–117
Merchant banking, ... 118–119
Money market accounts, ... 120–121
- account reconciliation and, ... 5
- business, ... 33, 34–35, 191
- corporate and municipal bonds and, ... 27
- foreign exchange and, ... 73
- individually managed portfolios and, ... 91
- investment management and, ... 101
- life insurance and, ... 113, 115
- pension fund and, ... 151
- portfolio management and, ... 159
- trust services and, ... 197
- wills and, ... 205

Money market deposit account, ... 3
Money market depository, checking or, ... 97, 99, 175
Money market fund
- general, ... 78–79, 122-123
- tax-free, ... 186–187
- U.S. government, ... 198–199

Money order, ... 124–125
Mortgages
- adjustable-rate, ... 8-9
- biweekly, ... 64
- commercial, ... 44–45
- construction loans and, ... 47, 153
- fixed-rate, ... 68–69
- graduated payment, ... 68
- land loan and, ... 109
- refinancing, ... 85, 87, 89
- second, ... 86, 172–173

Municipal bond fund, ... 126–127
Municipal department, ... 128–129
Mutual funds, ... 130–131
- acting as trustee and, ... 7
- aggressive growth, ... 10–11
- asset allocation, ... 14–15
- balanced, ... 22–23
- bond, ... 27, 28–29, 66-67

Mutual funds, (continued)
    brokerage services and, ... 31
    certificates of deposit and, ... 37
    custodial accounts and, ... 49
    estate planning services and, ... 61
    estate settlement services and, ... 59
    growth, ... 10-11, 80–81
    growth and/or income; see Growth and/or income mutual funds
    investment management and, ... 101
    offshore, ... 77, 95, 119
    option income, ... 140–141
    personal trust service and, ... 157
    portfolio management and, ... 159
    private banking and, ... 161
    stock, ... 27, 66–67

N
Night depository bags, ... 132–133
Notary public, ... 134–135
NOW account, ... 136–137
NYCE, ... 20

O
Offshore mutual funds, ... 77, 95, 119
On-line balance reporting, ... 138–139
    asset-based lending and, ... 17
    electronic banking interface and, ... 53
    electronic depository transfer and, ... 55
    employee-benefits services and, ... 57
    factoring and, ... 63
    foreign exchange and, ... 73
On-line balance reporting, (continued)
    forward contracts and, ... 71
    international fund administration and, ... 97
    international letter of credit and, ... 99
    late deposit window and, ... 111
    ship registration and, ... 175
    sweep investment account and, ... 185
Option income fund, ... 140–141
Overdraft protection, ... 142–143
    automatic teller machine cards and, ... 21
    bank-by-mail and, ... 25
    certificates of deposit and, ... 37
    checking (current) account and, ... 39
    direct deposit and, ... 51

Overdraft protection, (continued)
    individually managed portfolios and, .91
    individual retirement account and, ...93
    Mastercard/Visa and, ...117
    money market account and, ...121
    NOW account and, ...137

P

Passbook loans, ...144–145
Passbook savings, ...145, 146–147
Payroll services
    direct deposit, ...5, 207
    employee bond purchases and, ...148–149
    forward contracts and, ...71
    on-line balance sheet reporting and, ...139
    processing of, ...191
    simplified employee pension and, ...177
    zero balance account, ...209
Pension fund, ...150–151
    see also Keogh plans; Simplified employee pension
Personal line of credit, ...154–155, 142
Personal loan, ...103, 107
Portfolio management, ...158–159
    acting as trustee and, ...7
    brokerage services and, ...31
    custodial accounts and, ...49
    estate planning services and, ...61
    estate settlement services and, ...59
    personal trust service and, ...157
    private banking and, ...161
    wills and, ...205
Privacy, ...212

R

Rates of return, annual, ...218–219
Refinancing, ...85, 87, 89
Retirement account
    aggressive growth fund and, ...11
    asset allocation fund and, ...15
    balanced fund and, ...23
    bond mutual funds and, ...29, 67
    equity-income fund and, ...67
    growth and income fund and, ...83
    growth fund and, ...81
    money market fund and, ...79, 123

Retirement account (continued)
- municipal bond fund and, ...127
- mutual funds and, ...131
- option income fund and, ...141
- tax-free money market fund and, ...187
- U.S. government money market fund and, ...199

Revolving line of credit, ...55, 162–163
Right to privacy, ...212

S

Safe deposit box, ...147, 164–165
Salomon Brothers Long-Term, High-Grade Corporate Bond Index, ...218
Savings accounts, ...166–167
- automatic teller machine cards and, ...21
- certificates of deposit and, ...37
- direct deposit and, ...51
- individual retirement account (IRA) and, ...93
- Mastercard/Visa and, ...117
- money order and, ...125
- notary public and, ...135
- traveler's checks and, ...193
- treasurer's checks and, ...195

Savings bank life insurance, ...168–169
Ship registration, ...174–175
Simplified employee pension, ...176–177
Sinquefield, Rex A., ...219
Second mortgage, ...86, 172–173
Small business administration loan, ...170–171
Small-business line of credit, ...171, 178–179
Smeets, Christopher G., ...212
Standard & Poor's Composite Index, ...218
Standby letter of credit, ...180–181
Statement savings
- checking (current) account and, ...39
- money market account and, ...121
- night depository bags and, ...133
- NOW account and, ...137
- student loan and, ...183

Stock mutual funds, ...27, 66–67
Stocks, ...27, 30, 218, 219
Student loans, ...182–183
Sweep investment accounts, ...184–185
- account analysis and, ...3
- account reconciliation and, ...5

Sweep investment accounts, (continued)
    forward contracts and, ...71
    investment management and, ...101
    late deposit window and, ...111
    life insurance and, ...113
    payroll bonds processing and, ...149
    portfolio management and, ...159
    treasury, tax, and loan deposit (TTL) and, ...191
    zero balance account, ...209

T

Tax advice
    administration of companies and, .77
    individually managed portfolios and, ...91
    Internal Revenue Service reporting service and, ...105
    international business companies and, ...95
    merchant banking and, ...119
Tax-free money market fund, ...186–187
Tax services, ...188–189
1099, electronic or magnetic filing of, ...104
Time deposits, ...13, 36–37
Traveler's checks, ...192–193
Treasurer's checks, ...194–195
Treasury, tax, and loan deposit (TLL), ...190–191
Trust companies, ...30
Trustee, acting as, ...6
Trust services, ...196–197
    acting as trustee and, ...7
    aggressive growth fund and, ...11
    asset allocation fund and, ...15
    balanced fund and, ...23
    bond mutual funds and, ...29, 67
    brokerage services and, ...31
    equity-income fund and, ...67
    growth and income fund and, ...83
    growth fund and, ...81
    personal, ...156–157
    merchant banking and, ...119
    money market fund and, ...79, 123
    municipal bond fund and, ...127
    mutual funds and, ...131
    option income fund and, ...141
    simplified employee pension and, ...177
    tax-free money market fund and, ...187

Trust services, (continued)
- tax services and, ...189
- U.S. government money market fund and, ...199

U
U.S. government money market fund, ...198–199
U.S. savings bonds, ...148, 200–201
U.S. Treasury bills, rates of return for, ...218, 219

V
Vehicle dealership financing, ...202–203

W
Wills, ...204–205
Wire transfers, ...206–207
W2, electronic or magnetic filing of, ...104

Y
Yield, calculation of bond, ...26

Z
Zero balance account, ...208–209

Other Business-Related Books by Dwight S. Ritter

Branch Banking for the Nineties
Prentice Hall, Englewood, New Jersey

The Communicative Experience
Allyn & Bacon, Boston, Massachusetts

Cross Selling Financial Services
Wiley & Sons, New York, New York

High Performance Branch Banking
Irwin Professional, Chicago, Illinois

International Retail Banking
Lafferty Publications, Dublin, Ireland

Profit Economics
Boston University School of Management
Boston, Massachusetts

Relationship Banking
Irwin Professional, Chicago, Illinois

La Venta de Servicios Financieros
Ediciones Deusto S.A., Bilbao, Spain

Les Galaxies
de la Science-fiction

HERBERT
La maison des mères

Les Planètes
de la Science-Fantasy

McCAFFREY
Le dragon blanc

Les Univers
de la Fantasy

MOORCOCK
La quête de Tanelorn

Les Abîmes
de la Dark Fantasy

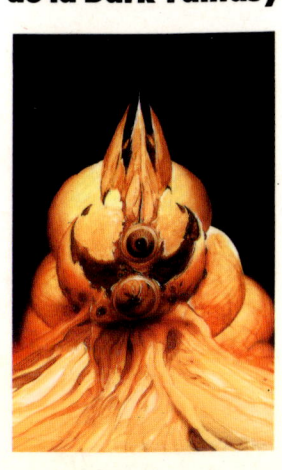

LOVECRAFT
La trace de Cthulhu